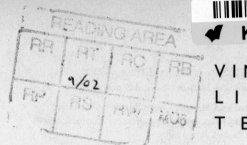

KT-448-855

VINTAGE LIVING TEXTS

Sebastian Faulks

THE ESSENTIAL GUIDE TO CONTEMPORARY LITERATURE

V

VINTAGE

Published by Vintage 2002

2 4 6 8 10 9 7 5 3 1

First published in Great Britain in 2002 by Vintage
Random House, 20 Vauxhall Bridge Road,
London SW1V 2SA

Random House Australia (Pty) Limited
20 Alfred Street, Milsons Point, Sydney,
New South Wales 2061, Australia

Random House New Zealand Limited
18 Poland Road, Glenfield,
Auckland 10, New Zealand

Random House (Pty) Limited
Endulini, 5A Jubilee Road, Parktown 2193, South Africa

The Random House Group Limited Reg. No. 954009
www.randomhouse.co.uk

A CIP catalogue record for this book is available from the British Library

ISBN 0099437562

Papers used by Random House are natural, recyclable products made
from wood grown in sustainable forests; the manufacturing processes
conform to the environmental regulations of the country of origin.

Typeset by Palimpsest Book Production Limited, Polmont, Stirlingshire

Printed and bound in Great Britain by
Bookmarque Ltd, Croydon, Surrey

CONTENTS

VINTAGE LIVING TEXTS: PREFACE

SEBASTIAN FAULKS

VINTAGE LIVING TEXTS

Birdsong

Charlotte Gray

The Girl at the Lion d'Or

VINTAGE LIVING TEXTS: REFERENCE

Acknowledgements

We owe grateful thanks to all at Random House. Most of all our debt is to Caroline Michel and her team at Vintage – especially Marcella Edwards – who have given us generous and unfailing support. Thanks also to Philippa Brewster and Georgina Capel, Michael Meredith, Angela Leighton, Harriet Marland, Louisa Joyner, Zara Warshal, to all our colleagues, and to our partners and families. We would also like to thank the teachers and students at schools and colleges around the country who have taken part in our trialling process, and who have responded so readily and warmly to our requests for advice. And finally, our thanks to Sebastian Faulks for his work, without whom . . . without which . . .

Preface

About this series

Vintage Living Texts: The Essential Guide to Contemporary Literature is a new concept in reading guides. Our aim is to provide readers of all kinds with an intelligent and accessible introduction to key works of contemporary literature. Each guide suggests techniques for reading important contemporary novels, and offers a variety of back-up materials that will give you ways into the text – without ever telling you what to think.

Content

All the books reproduce an extensive interview with the author, conducted exclusively for this series. This is not to say that we believe that the author's word is law. Of course it isn't. Once his or her book has gone out into the world he or she becomes simply yet another – if singularly competent – reader. This series recognises that an author's contribution may be valuable, and intriguing, but it puts the reader in control.

Every title in the series is author-focused and covers at least

I

three of their novels, along with relevant biographical, bibliographical, contextual and comparative material.

How to use this series

In the reading activities that make up the core of each book you will see that you are asked to do two things. One comes from the text; that is, we suggest what you should focus on, whether it's a theme, the language or the narrative method. The other concentrates on your own response. We want you to think about how you are reading and what skills you are bringing to bear in doing that reading. So this part is very much about you, the reader.

The point is that there are many ways of responding to a text. You could concentrate on the methods you might use to compare this text with others. In that case, look for the sections headed 'Compare'. Or you might want to do something more individual, and analyse how you are reacting to a text and what it means to you, in which case, pick out the approaches labelled 'Imagine' or 'Ask Yourself'.

Of course, it may well be that you are reading these texts for an exam. In that case you will have to go for the more traditional methods of literary criticism and look for the responses that tell you to 'Discuss' or 'Analyse'. Whichever level you (or your students) are at, you will find that there is something here for everyone. But we're not suggesting that you stick solely to the approaches we offer, or that you tackle all of the exercises laid out here. Choose whatever most interests you, or whatever best suits your purposes.

Who are these books for?

Students will find that these guides are like a good teacher. They introduce the life and work of the author, set each novel in its context, explain key ideas and literary critical terms as they arise, suggest comparative exercises in a number of media, and ask focused questions to encourage a well-informed, analytical approach to reading the novels in a way that is rigorous, but still entertaining.

Teachers will find in this series a rich source of ideas for teaching contemporary novels and their contexts, particularly at AS, A and undergraduate level. The exercises on each text have been tailored to meet the various assessment objectives laid down in the subject criteria for GCE AS and GCE A Level English Literature, and are explained in such a way that they can easily be selected and fitted into a lesson plan. Given the diversity of ways in which the awarding bodies have devised their specifications to meet these assessment objectives, a wide range of exercises is offered. We've had fun devising the plans, and we hope they'll be fun for you when you come to teach and learn with them.

And if you are neither a teacher nor a student of contemporary literature, but someone reading for your own pleasure? Well, if you've ever wanted someone to introduce you to a novelist's work in a way that will let you trust your own judgement and read more confidently, then this guide is also for you.

Whoever you are, we hope that you will enjoy using these books and that they will send you back to the novels to find new pleasures.

All page references in this text refer to the Vintage edition.

Sebastian Faulks

Introduction

When we interviewed Sebastian Faulks for this book we asked him a question about letters. Why was it that so many letters in his novels were misdirected, misdelivered, failed to reach the right person, were not read by the right person and – in some cases – were only imagined, so that they never even got written in the first place? As you'll see if you look this question up, Faulks was not even sure what we were talking about. He hadn't noticed all these lost letters.

Of course there are also many letters that do get sent and do get read. But these thwarted missives suggest something telling about the preoccupations in Faulks's novels and hint at a number of his themes. In one way it's not surprising that there are so many letters in Faulks, because the device of using letters in novels and inserting their text into the narrative is one that makes for solidity – a pretend concrete reality. This is what this character said to this other character, without the mediation of the narrating voice or the intervention of any other character's perspective. The author has created – made up – this letter, but we are willing temporarily to believe in its existence and its truth as an imaginative reality.

Many critics and reviewers have commented on Faulks's

ability to create an imagined world that seems to have a solid existence. He does this by doing an extensive amount of historical research, as his 'Author's Note' to *Charlotte Gray* tells us. As a result, reviewers like to play the 'spot the error' game with Faulks's books. Sometimes they do find tiny discrepancies. Sometimes they think they know more about the past that they imagine they remember, than they do about the past that Faulks has recovered through research. When he was writing *On Green Dolphin Street* (2001) his editor got very worried about the statement that there were banks of television screens on Pennsylvania Station in the 1960s. 'No,' said the editor, 'that's too early for television – you've made a mistake.' In fact, the screens were there, but Faulks did decide to take the detail out because it was clearly only going to become a continuing slur on his historical accuracy.

But it is the tiny details that do most of the work in creating Faulks's other worlds: details about food, details about houses, details about the weather and details about clothes. In the interview that follows, Faulks speaks intriguingly about how houses 'really really get me going', but to us it's the food and the clothes that dominate – especially, interestingly, the women's clothes. Given that Faulks is dealing with period settings in *The Girl at the Lion d'Or* (in this case, 1936), in *Birdsong* (1910–18 and 1978–9), in *Charlotte Gray* (1942–3) and in *On Green Dolphin Street* (1959–60), it is crucial that he should be able to convey the atmosphere of those worlds and it is through these details that he does so. It's an interesting method. The minutiae of this information works on us because we can draw on a shared experience; clothes and food are just as important to each one of us now as they are to characters in novels. But the difference in what we know in our lives about the clothes we wear and the food we eat, compared to those that appear in that strange world inhabited by these characters, creates a tension that sets the scene. In this way a connection is made between 'us' and 'them', but it's one that is slightly surreal, given that most of us never have and never will wear those kinds of clothes or eat quite that sort of food.

In spite of all those lost letters, there are other ways in which Faulks makes connections. In the novels of the French trilogy there are a number of characters who come back into stories that are not – strictly speaking – their own. Charles Hartmann appears in all three novels. Levi appears in *Birdsong* and *Charlotte Gray*. William Gray appears in *Birdsong*, and becomes quite an important character in *Charlotte Gray*. The other way round, Stephen Wraysford, the hero of *Birdsong*, is mentioned briefly in *Charlotte Gray*.

It is, as Faulks says, a good game for the reader, but it is more than that. The interweaving of the novels, the crossing over of characters, helps to remind us that human beings are never alone. The actions of one individual can rebound on another, and the consequences of those actions can carry on down the years, to come out in quite another, and unexpected, place. This is – to some extent – the point of the 1970s' 'Elizabeth' episodes that punctuate *Birdsong*. More than that, the larger actions of a society, or a government, can (and do) affect the lives of millions, and dictate the events of people's experiences, generation after generation. It is a sobering aspect of the history of the twentieth century that this is the case. The effect of the First World War on Faulks's fictional characters is great. But he is reflecting an important truth about history, and about the degree to which we are all – still – affected by that history. In *Birdsong* Stephen writes in his journal, 'No child or future generation will ever know what this was like. They will never understand' (p. 422). Maybe they won't, maybe they never can if they have not lived through it, but Faulks's method and his message suggest that it is our responsibility to try.

Connection and memory are two key themes in Faulks's

novels. But this memory is not always something that can be told precisely. For all the concrete details, for all the solid houses and meals, there is always something just out of reach in the memory of his characters. It's a delicate technique. Sebastian Faulks speaks of being interested in memory that is 'just outside my power to recall', just beyond the grasp of consciousness or reason. There is a 'feeling' or 'instinctive' tone in many of these novels – a tone that some critics have identified as 'feminine'. It's true that Faulks does often focus on women: think of Isabelle and Jeanne, Anne and Charlotte. But it's also true that his work focuses on the subtle and fluctuating relationships between parents and children, as well as on the relations between lovers – men and women – and between comrades in arms, whether Stephen and Weir, or Charlotte and Julien. Nothing lasts because everything changes. But that *is* what lasts: that everything changes. And while this is the case, there can be no hard rules, universal truths, or whole explanations. There can only be an attention to consciousness in the moment, and an attempt to understand in the moment.

'Disappearing' is an important word in Faulks's *Charlotte Gray*. It is a word that goes with other instances where things are being lost or undone. As Levade expires, death is a 'rapid, sweet unravelling'. Charlotte – and Isabelle and Stephen in *Birdsong* – experience a loss of self in physical passion, which becomes, paradoxically, the centre of their identity. In an important passage in *Birdsong*, Stephen, boating down the Somme with Isabelle and her family, is assaulted by desire, and the knowing narrative, and the knowing reader, understand the allusion, the reference to what is to come:

Stephen tried to drag his mind from the vision of decay the river had induced. The pressure of Madame Azaire's foot against his leg slowly increased until most of her calf rested against him. The

simple frisson this touch had earlier given to his
charged senses now seemed complicated; the sensation of desire seemed indistinguishable from an
impulse towards death. (p. 45)

Dissolution and disappearance are the themes of Faulks's novels.
Set against this is only the self-consciousness of the examined
life, and the recording of that life having been lived – in memorials, in art, in novels. These continue to be major themes. Faulks
published the last volume of his French trilogy in 1998. He says
that he might go back to France. However, for now, he has
transposed these same themes into a more recent past, and a
different place. *On Green Dolphin Street* is set in America and
England in the late 1950s and early 1960s, but Faulks's readers
will recognise his anxieties and his strengths. In *On Green Dolphin
Street* it's 1959 and Mary is living in Washington:

She took a table in the corner, and looked out of
the window, towards the river and the Theodore
Roosevelt Memorial. Few cities in the world could
have had so many memorials in proportion to such
a relatively short lifetime, she thought. Without
thinking too hard, she could list the lapidary
reminders of Lincoln, Jefferson, Roosevelt; the
George Washington Memorial Parkway, the George
Mason Memorial Bridge, the Arlington Memorial
Bridge leading to the Iwo Jima Marine Corps
Memorial . . . What were they so scared of forgetting? (p. 41)

The answer must be: forgetfulness itself. Only through memory
and memorials can the effects of the past be explained in the
present. And the connection must be made if there is to be
any responsibility.

9

Much of the connection that goes on in Sebastian Faulks's novels is up to us – the readers – to supply. At the end of *On Green Dolphin Street* the lovers whose story it is, Frank and Mary, are on the verge of separation. In an extended episode Mary leaves, but then we see Frank change his mind and go after her. The traffic is terrible; he crawls along towards the airport watching the clock, cursing. Her plane is scheduled to take off at this time. The moment passes. She is gone. He weeps. Then we hear Mary's story. She leaves. We see her change her mind and decide to call him. The phone rings in the empty apartment. She keeps trying. Her flight is delayed – there is still time – she keeps trying. No answer. She gets on the plane. She weeps.

It's a story about a failure of connection, about loss and lost chances. But neither Mary nor Frank knows what we know. That they both tried to find each other across that void. That the connection could have been made. Faulks is sterner than to give in to our wish for a happy ending, but in the mind of the reader the story is resolved.

Interview with Sebastian Faulks

London: 21 August 2001

BIRDSONG

JN: Could you tell us what was the germ of the idea for *Birdsong*?

SF: It goes back to when I was a child at school, at the age of about eleven or twelve, the first time I really heard about the war. The schoolmaster who was teaching English also taught us pretty much everything else as well, and was a very knowledgeable man, we rather looked up to him. When it came to talking about the First World War, he was able to give us dates and facts, but he didn't seem able to put across what it was really like. He said things like 'It was simply indescribable' . . . 'You don't really want to know about it – we don't want to think about it'. And I remember thinking at that time: that's remarkable . . . and I just stored that at the back of my mind.

And at the same time, at the same school, on Remembrance Sunday some boy would read out the names of all the old boys of the school who had died in these two wars, and one year it was my turn to do it. I remember being enormously struck by the sheer number of names – it just went on and on and on, and it was a very small school, only eighty boys, I think.

There probably would have been fewer than that at the relevant time. The list just seemed to go on for ever. So those two things stuck in the back of my mind.

Many years later, I was writing my second novel, *The Girl at the Lion d'Or*, which is set in 1936. It is about a young woman in a provincial town in France who had had a trauma in childhood, and because she was only about twenty at the time, and 1936 was a sort of given and I couldn't change that, it meant that her childhood would have been in and around the First World War and the end of it. And it was a sort of Pandora's box that I didn't particularly want to open, because there was a lot of background of France in the 'thirties and I didn't really want to go back into that First World War because it seemed too big a subject. But eventually I concluded that I had to a bit, and so I read a book by Alistair Horne about Verdun, about the French experience of the First World War. I was immensely struck by the details, really, of the day-to-day life of the soldiers. And I took what I needed from it to use in *The Girl at the Lion d'Or,* but I thought . . . hmm, I want to know more about this.

Then in 1988, which was the seventieth anniversary of the Armistice, a great flood of books came out about it, and I read quite a few of those. There was one in particular I came across called *War Underground,* which was the story of the tunnellers who tunnelled underneath no-man's-land. I'd no idea that this tunnelling had taken place, and it seemed to me a very suggestive thing that beneath this inferno there was an even deeper, smaller, more horrific – in some ways a more horrific – world.

One of the problems of writing a novel set in the First World War was that although I felt that many people are quite ignorant about it, people of my generation had rather my view: 'Terrible thing, appalling thing, massive slaughters . . . whew . . . you know . . .' but didn't really know much more than that.

At the same time, it was a war that produced great literature – poetry particularly, but also memoirs and so on – and there were many people who were extremely well informed about it. So there was a paradox, and the only way that I could see round it was by writing a book which dealt with it very head-on – and it was always going to be a very head-on, operatic sort of book. The only way I could get over people saying 'Yes, yes, we know all this' was to tell them something that they *didn't* know. The tunnellers provided me with a way in, and once I'd got that I got lots of suggestive details that played in quite well to the themes that were developing in my mind.

Another given about writing a novel about the First World War was that I wanted to write about the area *before* it became known as the battlefield. I've always been rather fascinated by this idea that the Somme was once a river without this awful connotation – just as Hiroshima and Auschwitz were just ordinary places, before anything horrible happened there. So I had a pre-war beginning and I had the 'something new', as it were, that I was going to tell, and those were the key things. Then there were lots of other technical difficulties about how to get it going, and which battles to choose.

Those were the germs, and from those grew the main theme of the book. In the research I was doing, the thing that occurred to me again and again was the simple question of 'Why didn't anyone stop this?' Why didn't someone say, 'Actually I can't just hold this machine gun any longer and tap it gently from side to side and kill . . . ten, twenty, thirty, forty, fifty . . . tap it again . . . eighty, ninety . . . tap it again . . . a hundred, a hundred and twenty . . . I can't do this.' But nobody did. There were mutinies, it's true to say, in all the armies, but there seemed to be no lengths to which human beings could not be driven. And that was the working title of the book, 'How far can you go?' Of course I wasn't really seriously going to call it that, but that was the idea.

JN: Taking that idea of 'how far can you go?' – the novel seems to be pushing more and more towards the idea that the experience of war is meaningless, when human beings will go that far, push beyond all limits. Does the novel set out to assert the value of any redeeming features in human nature, to set against the meaninglessness of the experience of war?

SF: Not really. I think that it's the function of birdsong – which is something that occurs at various stages in the book, and which I came across endlessly in research – that even in the midst of this awful slaughter you suddenly found that there'd be a fox snuffling around, or you'd hear a lark singing, and it underlines nature's utter indifference to human beings and what they do. But there's also a sense that humanity is indifferent to itself because it simply continues anyway, and the birth that ends the book is, to some extent, a redemption, by naming the child who is born after the child who has died in the book. It is a gesture of redemption by one character in the book towards another who has died, but what's really happened is that animate beings have bred as they will always breed, given any sort of circumstances, and there isn't really meant to be any sort of tremendous message of hope, or anything more than just that.

JN: God is only felt as an absence in the novel. Even those characters who start as believers lose their faith along the way. Those who put their trust in love feel betrayed by it. Is there a sense, do you think, in which our society has lost faith in God or in love, *because* of the First World War? Is there a lasting effect?

SF: Well, maybe. I'm not enough of a historian to know. But it's not quite right to say that God is felt only as an absence. In the case of Jack, the miner, his response is very logical, in that he firmly believes, and then he sees things that destroy his belief and he ends up by disbelieving: as a reasonable man would. Also the chaplain whom he watches the first day of the battle of the Somme: he just tears off his cross – he can no longer believe this. That's actually based on an eye-witness account. But Stephen, paradoxically, is perverse really. In some ways he becomes *more* spiritual as the book goes on. I wouldn't say he becomes a believer in any sense, but the more incomprehensible and baffling it becomes, the more curious he is about it. He wants to know how far you can go, and he becomes more open to the idea of some divine plan, although it's never fully realised in his mind.

I do think that historically, certainly, the First World War saw the beginning of the end of a loss of belief in *authority*, and whether that is divine authority, or political or class authority, I don't really know enough to say. But certainly you feel it now. It's a continuing process, it's changed since when I was a child. I was born in 1953. There was still an automatically given respect towards the Church, teachers, doctors, lawyers, the law, the courts and all that. This has eroded, in my belief, faster in the last twenty years than in the previous twenty or thirty. But no one has *given* authority any more. There is no automatic respect for position. Each individual within a position has to *earn* respect by his or her actions, it seems to me. And obviously many of the structures contributed to their own downfall.

Traditionally the view is that the First World War was the watershed at which this whole process began. And you have to say that it was an inevitable thing, and I think in large measure a good thing: not to follow unquestioningly into death, for no purpose. Though again there are counter-arguments that there was a purpose. I mean a Europe and a Middle East and a Russia dominated by the Kaiser would have been a less nice place to live, though it wasn't much of a place to live in the 'twenties and 'thirties anyway.

Certainly the people who fought in the Second World War were much more unillusioned and they went more knowingly, more sardonically, reluctantly, and more critically – I think – of the politicians who had failed them. But without that necessary kowtowing to authority.

JN: You're very interested in places. You've already talked about France: France before the war, France after the war – places that provide security, the idea of home. I think in particular of the red room which Isabelle promised Stephen would always be there, but in fact of course is bombed. And the fact that Stephen has no home, nor indeed does Isabelle, a home they could genuinely go to. What is the meaning of a sense of place to you?

SF: It's interesting you use the word 'home'. There's another book I wrote, called *The Fool's Alphabet*, which is entirely about this, actually. It's set in twenty-six different places. It's like an A to Z – it begins with a place beginning with A and ends in a place beginning with Z – and it's about what places mean in a man's life, and the word 'home' doesn't appear in the book until the very last word, so that's very germane to what you're saying.

Places are very much part of the initial throb of the idea for me. I couldn't say, 'I'll write a story or a book whose themes are this, this and this, and whose characters are going to be this, this and this. I might set it in Australia, or I might set it in London, or it might be Paraguay, I'm not quite sure yet.' That never happens to me. Paraguay, or Australia, or wherever, is absolutely part of the initial throb of the whole thing, and it becomes a main character in the book. I don't quite know why this is, it's just that that's how it comes to me, and in a sense it's not really in my hands.

I am very fascinated by houses in particular. I find houses really really get me going. I was a bit stuck in *Charlotte Gray*, and I went to see some friends of mine who were on holiday – we were living in France at the time – and as soon as I went into their house, which was a rather old, slightly decrepit manor, it all kick-started again. This was the house in which Charlotte could go and lodge, and work as a cleaner. I just spent the whole afternoon in a sort of daze, wandering around this place. It wasn't merely that I tried to capture the atmosphere of that house, but the house itself suggested incidents which might happen inside it. I suppose, for me, that is the real function of place. I have no compunction at all about taking houses out of real life and putting them in books, almost unchanged.

Whereas with characters, I don't do that at all. I feel that would be a really bad practice, and wouldn't work. For the simple reason that if you create a completely credible world, which I go to great pains to do, in a rather builderish, structural way – if you then take someone from another world (i.e. our world), and put them in there, they don't work. In the same way that in our world, if you suddenly tell a lie, it generally doesn't work: people sniff you out. So it's really bad practice to take people from real life. Of course I will take the odd verbal tic, or I'll take the colour of someone's eyes or something, but that's about it. I'm quite unusual in this, I believe.

But the same is not true with places. In *The Girl at the Lion d'Or* the main house there is absolutely from real life. In *Charlotte Gray* likewise. In *Birdsong* the house with the red room is taken from life. I'd never been inside the room at the time I was writing. I have subsequently been inside, and it's actually remarkably like . . . [chuckles]. Actually the gentleman who owns it is a very proper, superior merchant type, I would say, and he was extremely shocked by the book, and took a lot of teasing, and people suggested, 'Your granny was a bit fast.' And he kept showing me around and saying, 'As you can see, it's really not at all like it is in your book.' And I'm saying, 'No, no, not at all.' When it was *absolutely* the spitting image . . . It was slightly smaller, and there weren't as many corridors. But I knew that I'd enlarged it.

But back to the idea of home. I suppose there is a recurrent idea of a lost home, isn't there? And that, I suppose, must be something quite deep in me, but I am not quite sure what it is. But I'm very fascinated by those parts of my life which are just outside my power to recall. In other words, both the years before I became able to recall continuously – so one till five, whatever it might be. And also things I feel I've half-forgotten, or half-dreamed, I'm not quite sure about, but I wish were still there, and I've somehow lost, and can't quite recover. But the sense that they do still exist – and this also ties into the question of time – the fact that everything passes, doesn't mean to say that nothing lasts. And this is touched on in *Birdsong* when Stephen is reunited with Isabelle, and he's able to convince himself that although, in some temporal sense, their love affair is over because they're physically separated, if feeling has existed at one time, the physical separation and the movement of time don't mean to say that the feeling is extinct. It's put terribly plainly and violently in the book I'm reading at the moment, which is *The Human Stain* by Philip Roth, and it goes something like 'Because nothing lasts, nothing changes . . . *because* nothing lasts, everything remains.'

CHARLOTTE GRAY

JN: While you were talking about experience which lies just outside of memory, I was thinking of *Charlotte Gray*, because clearly that's a theme that runs through that book – the memory she can't quite reach until the end. How self-consciously did you develop the hints about that idea leading towards the revelation, or were you yourself unsure quite what the experience would be?

SF: I knew what the experience was, but it was very tricky. I wanted to suggest that it was something powerful and important that she couldn't quite remember. You're obviously going into recovered memory, and we all know what that is about. And I tried not to mislead people into thinking that she'd been sexually abused. But at the same time I did leave it open. What I was trying to do was to suggest in a sense that the way in which he abused her – by trying to offload his experiences on to her, on to the shoulders of a small child – was in a sense an abuse almost worse than some physical or sexual thing. In my mind it was clear what it was. But part of the problem, of course, is that it's a very abstract thing to suggest to people – the transfer of some emotional weight from your shoulders to someone else's is very difficult to explain. And also I knew that the climactic scene of the book, in a way, would be the moment at which she is reconciled with her father. But what happens in real life is that this kind of psychological cleansing, which is what it is, takes place over an extremely long time. It takes a very long time for anyone to dig the stuff up, understand it, come to terms with it, stand back from it and then purge it, and then it runs clear.

This would probably take years, in real life. But dramatically the demands of the book are that it has to be done within a chapter and the climax of it has to done within a scene, and this was extraordinarily difficult to pull off without seeming trite. But at the same time you can't drag readers through three years. So it was terribly difficult to do, and therefore I had to fuzz it a bit around the edges, so that it didn't seem too pat. And the literary judgement therefore is that you've got to deliver: you can't pull the punch, you've got to deliver. But at

19

the same time, you've got to say to the more sophisticated reader, 'Yes . . . I do understand that life isn't really quite like that', and therefore you have to blur it a little bit around the edges, to make it sort of bleed away a bit.

JN: Do you find it more difficult to write from a woman's point of view?

SF: I *don't* really. Well, I suppose I must find it a *bit* more difficult, mustn't I? But the sex of the character is, in most scenes, not really the dominant thing that's in your mind. In most scenes the dominant thing is what you want to convey in the scene, and in most scenes the psychology and temperament of the individual, the age of the individual, and obviously the circumstances in which they find themselves – their nationality, the kind of person they are, the stress they're under or not, the historical era in which they're living – all these will count for considerably more than whether they're male or female. So in most scenes it's not really a very big deal, in my view. Secondly, because you've created them both man and woman, you know them, and if you don't understand them, who else is going to?

In all of my books the scenes are only ever told from one point of view, even though you're itching to give the other person's, you have to let that come later. This is a fairly elementary technique, which was explained to me by my first editor and which I've stuck with, and it does work. I will go back at the end of the scene, if it's been a woman, and say, Hmm, okay, well, Mary or Charlotte, or whoever it's been, has got through this scene in exactly the way that I want, but has she in the course of this scene done something which may be what I want her to do, or say, or think, but which in fact is not feasible for any woman to have done, said or thought? So it's like running an extra check through, it's like a spellcheck on your computer. Just occasionally I will tamper with it, or I will ask advice. My editor's a woman, my wife's a woman . . . and occasionally they've said, 'Yes, why doesn't she . . . ? Isn't she more interested in this or that, or . . . ?'

I've talked to women novelists about this and they've been quite robust in their criticisms – not actually of me though. Pat Barker I once heard being quite robust in her criticism of a male writer whose female character was being abducted in some strange way. And the male writer had her concerns being about this, that or the other, and Pat Barker said, 'There's only two things she will be worried about: (1) Will I be raped, and (2) if so, will I be pregnant?' She said there is absolutely no woman in the world who would have any other thoughts. I was very interested in hearing her say this. I do run that sort of Pat Barker check through my mind, too. I think, well, is there a primal thing here I'm missing, because I'm so interested in the specific psychology of my character? Is there a basic thing I'm missing here?

I do like writing inside a woman's mind. People ask me about it all the time, so I suppose I have thought about it a lot, and there is a certain way which helps me – this is a terrible generalisation – but women seem to be more continuously attentive to the variations of their own responses than men are: to value them more highly and weigh them more continuously. If a book you're writing is about gradual changes of emotional and psychological position, it's sometimes more feasible to have the majority or a very large part of it told through a woman's eyes. I'm not saying that men are no good at introspection – but I suppose that in my books it does seem that way. If you look at *Birdsong*, Stephen is not given to introspection (I think that phrase is even used); in *On Green Dolphin Street* Frank is not given to introspection. Charley, the husband, is given to introspection, but in a morbid way, and in a morbid and intellectual way rather than in an emotional way. And it gives you a kind of dramatic conflict, I suppose.

JN: In *Charlotte Gray* you set up passion and logical argument as two contrasting avenues to truth, or two different kinds of truth. Am I right in thinking that your novels explore and celebrate the truth of passion above the truth of logical, rational thought?

SF: That's a big and rather abstract question. I do think that I have a romantic view of life, in the sense that – what we were talking about just now – the fact that experiences are no longer continuing doesn't mean to say that they lose their validity. Because if you judge the validity of something by whether it endures and lasts or not, then everything is worthless because nothing lasts, so therefore you have to think of different criteria. I'm unable to discern any logical meaning in existence. I'm unable, logically, to understand the conditions of existence. I don't understand space, time . . . the whole thing seems to me in some logical sense a contradiction in terms. I don't understand how it could be that we do exist. So I've long ago abandoned any search for meaning, but I do believe there are values, and I do believe experiences have value, and that one of the things I'm trying to do in writing novels is to look at those values. How they're formed, what they mean to people, and how they last, even after they have apparently finished, and how they can last through a person's life into another generation and how experiences of certain degrees of power will go on. Unfortunately, these may be negative experiences: the memory of war, the impact of loss, and so on. But also, as against that, I'm interested in the redemptive power of love, and memory and consolation. So I suppose it sounds rather as though I'm saying 'yes' to your question . . . But they are very logically worked-out books, and the process is logical and the organisation and the structure are logical. But logic is only a tool, isn't it? It's a very useful tool, but it's not the only one in the box.

JN: There's a theme in *Charlotte Gray* of works of art, literary works of art, visual works of art. And at certain points there is what looks almost like a manifesto for what art can do in capturing some transcendent truth. Would it be right to say that *Charlotte Gray* is partly about art, and what art can do?

SF: Actually it's a book that's got a hell of a lot in it. It's really packed with the idea of art at these transcendent moments redeeming and opening people's lives, and there is a sense in which the reading of Proust has done something for Charlotte. It has opened up to her the possibility of memory and the possibility of what memory can do, especially the operation of involuntary memory: can you reach out beyond what you actually remember, and if so, what will you find?

Not just in a psychological sense, also in an artistic sense. I was very struck by the painter called de Chirico, on whose work Levade's is slightly based. There's a long description of a painting in the book, which is supposed to suggest that. De Chirico lost the ability to paint, during the war . . . or after the war . . . or was it the other way around? I forget. Levade feels that art has failed him, or maybe he has failed art. There's another bit in Proust about the writer called Bergotte, whose death scene is redeemed by his going to see a view of Delft by Vermeer one more time. He's a failed writer, but somehow art has redeemed him.

There's a lot in *Charlotte Gray* about the ability of art to redeem people's lives and give value and meaning to them. It's quite loosely knitted in, but it knits into the themes of transcendence and memory and time. I haven't read the book for quite a long time. But I do remember that all these layers are supposed to pack into one another. Really, what the book is about is the extent to which a woman's life parallels the life of a country, and what Charlotte is trying to get back to is some Paradise, which may or may not be an actual one. To reconnect with a past, in the same way that France – which seems to have terribly lost its way – is trying to reconnect to a past. And that's the parallel of a woman and a country. But can France reconnect to that past? Did that past ever really exist anyway? And that is the function of what Julien does in the book. At least he keeps that thread intact. Then afterwards it's for him to discover whether that past was ever really there or not.

JN: There's a suggestion in *Charlotte Gray* of a similar crime, if you like, to the one of keeping shooting that you were talking about in *Birdsong*, and never saying, 'I won't do this' – that is the crime of turning a blind eye. You raise the question of why it is that decent people stood aside and let the Jews be rounded up during the Occupation and said nothing about it. Do you regard that as the major French betrayal of themselves?

SF: Yes, I think that's one of the major betrayals. The horrible thing about what happened is that much of the German Occupation was very welcome to a large number of French people, who viewed it as implementing domestic policies that they had long wanted to see. For many years afterwards there were still people who were strong Petainists. I mean, de Gaulle sold the country a sort of compromise to save it from civil war, and it was an untruth really, which was: 'I will march down the Champs-Elysées with the American army and we will have liberated France by force of arms, and you must believe in this, "La France Résistante"'. People bought into this happily.

In fact, two and a half per cent of the adult population were awarded some sort of medal in recognition of resistance work. The number involved in resistance work was approximately the same as the number involved in counter-resistance working for the Milice and other organisations, approximately two and half per cent of the population. So ninety-five per cent of the population did nothing one way or the other. That's pretty shameful. But this has to be seen through a long context, going back principally to the First World War, and the decimation of a whole generation of French men and the effect of that on French women, and society, and so on.

There's a way in which Julien is quite lucky and I think he recognised this himself, in so far as he would – like everyone else – have said that Pétain's original terms for the Armistice with Hitler were quite good. He got two-thirds of the country unoccupied, he got superior economic terms for Occupation, superior movement of citizens to any of the other occupied countries in Europe, and he said quite openly, '*J'entre dans la voie de la collaboration*' – 'we enter into the way of collaboration'. Collaboration was not a dirty word at the beginning. It was a synonym for cooperation. What else are you supposed to do when your country is overrun by force of arms? He'd done a reasonably good deal. The French policy of collaboration failed only because the Germans were not interested in collaborating with the French. They viewed them as *Untermenschen* in the same way that they viewed the Slavs and the Poles and everyone else. France could never believe this. The French *école normale supérieure* couldn't believe that anyone could view them as such trash, but they didn't understand the Nazi mind. Because the boss that Julien works for in Paris is Jewish and is humiliated and forced to wear the star, Julien thinks, 'Christ. This is not on. I can't allow this.' So it forces him to take up a kind of resistant attitude. But had he worked in another company where his boss had not been Jewish, had he worked in a sleepy town in the Loire valley where there wasn't much going on . . . Who's to know?

So one can't assume a morally superior attitude as a matter of course. There is a great deal of luck in all these things but a large number of French people had no idea that Jewish children were being rounded up to fulfil a quota, and they didn't know that the children had been offered specifically by Laval to fulfil that quota. The whole French state, by which I mean the workings of the civil service and everything, was utterly complicit in this. With the best will in the world, in response to 'Well, it's easier to go along with this, it's not my job, I'm only obeying orders . . .' somebody has really to say 'No'. I think more people should have said no, and I think more people could have said no. But it is complex.

JN: There's lots of miscommunication in *Charlotte Gray*, not just miscommunication through separation, through distance, but letters – letters that are not sent, letters than are torn up, letters that are misdirected. Is there any sense in which you mistrust communication between characters?

SF: No, I can't remember these letters particularly.

JN: Well, there are the letters that the Jewish children write, which are dumped on the station platform.

SF: That was just a cruel detail from research. What other letters were there?

JN: There were several other letters. Certainly in *Birdsong* there are masses of letters where Stephen will write a letter to somebody and think, no, that's no good and tear it up, and Isabelle does the same.

SF: I suppose so. I hadn't thought of it in any detailed way. Maybe I just read too much Thomas Hardy, I don't know. No,

I don't think I've got any deep thematic intention there . . .

JN: In *Charlotte Gray* you reintroduce a number of characters who were featured in *Birdsong*, usually major characters coming back in minor roles. What extra scope does this interweaving give you?

SF: Very little. It's merely a kind of pleasure, a small pleasure for the reader who's read all three, and *The Girl at the Lion d'Or* as well. I quite like it. You think, 'Oh, yes', just worlds touching one another. And it does give you the sense that each world has its own story, and you could have begun the novel in the room with the piano instead of in the room they're sitting in.

It's just a pleasant, readerly sort of thing. The main character in *The Girl at the Lion d'Or*, Hartmann, appears briefly in *Birdsong*, and then again in *Charlotte Gray*. He's the only character who appears in all three. And Levi, the German who rescues Stephen from the tunnel, appears again, with Hartmann, in Drancy in *Charlotte Gray*. And there is also actually a musical connection between *Birdsong* and *Charlotte Gray*, which is very, very slight – one for the real connoisseur! I don't think anyone has ever spotted it.

JN: Having written the French trilogy, why the shift to America in 1960 [in *On Green Dolphin Street*]?

SF: Well, I couldn't write . . . Well, I suppose I *could* write a tetralogy actually – I might come back to France.

VINTAGE
LIVING
TEXTS

Birdsong

IN CLOSE-UP

Reading guides for

BIRDSONG

BEFORE YOU BEGIN TO READ . . .

The novel depicts imaginary events in France in 1910, four years before the First World War started; events in France during the war in 1916–18; and events in England in 1978–9. Part One contrasts the war with the society that existed immediately before it, whose characters are ignorant of the cataclysm about to happen. Later parts juxtapose the war with modern Europe, where the characters are shown to know little of the events of 1914–18 that helped to shape the society they live in.

Look at the interview with Faulks, and read the section on *Birdsong*. You will see there that Faulks identifies a number of themes, including:

- War and its legacy
- Nature's indifference to human suffering
- Moral and political authority
- The idea of home
- Time and change

Other themes you might like to consider include:

- Trust and betrayal
- Sense of place
- The influence of history
- The boundaries of human behaviour
- Redemption

While you are reading *Birdsong*, *Charlotte Gray* and *The Girl at the Lion d'Or* in detail it is worth bearing these overall themes in mind. At the end of each detailed reading guide you will find suggested contexts, which will help you to situate the themes in relation to the novel as a whole. The reading activities given below are not designed to be followed slavishly. Choose whichever sections most interest you or are most useful for your own purposes. The questions that are set at the end of each chapter plan are to help you relate each individual chapter to the novel as a whole.

Reading activities: detailed analysis

PART ONE. FRANCE, 1910.
SECTIONS 1, 2, 3 and 4 (pp. 3–33)

Focus on: sense of place

ANALYSE . . .

— Consider the impression created of Amiens in 1910 in these opening sections. What atmosphere is suggested? Analyse which details create this atmosphere. In what ways is this a portrait of a way of life and of a regional landscape that have now gone?

— What sense of place is created by the descriptions of the Azaires' house in these sections? How does the suggestion of violence on p. 16 add to these impressions?

Focus on: characterisation

CONSIDER CHARACTERS IN CONTRAST TO THEIR SETTING . . .

— Think about how Isabelle Azaire is portrayed in these first four sections. In what ways does she seem out of place in that house and that social setting?

— How is Stephen's erotic interest in Isabelle suggested? What effects are created by the fact that her portrait is from his point of view? And what influence does her social environment have on the way they relate?

Focus on: themes

— Several themes are introduced in these opening sections, which will become centrally important later in the novel. Consider these themes:

- The theme of private conscience and public role. In what ways do these opening sections contrast characters' private consciences with their public roles?
- The theme of trust and betrayal. Isabelle claims to be 'loyal' to Azaire; does her behaviour bear this out? Stephen is not without guile in his advances; what are your impressions of him here? How do you react to the fact that Azaire's trust is being betrayed by his wife and his guest? What aspects of the text manipulate you to react in the ways that you do?
- The theme of religious faith. Compare Isabelle's 'act of Christian charity' (p. 32) with Aunt Élise's 'religious sensitivity' (p. 26). Which is the more sincere? The more valid? The more socially acceptable?

PART ONE
SECTION 5 (pp. 34–47)

Focus on: social context

ANALYSE GENDER ROLES . . .

— What impressions have you formed of the role of women in France in 1910 in the novel? Why does Isabelle not simply refuse to comply with others' expectations, and which social expectations seem to limit her power of independent action?

Focus on: symbolism

LOOK CLOSELY AT LANGUAGE . . .

— Examine the language used to describe the ambience of the family picnic on pp. 40–7. In what ways do the images symbolise aspects of the characters' lives, and the mood of their social group?

— The motif of birdsong is gradually developed, both as a literal background to events and as a richly suggestive symbol. What images and ideas have been associated with birdsong so far in the novel? As you read, make a note of all the images of song and birdsong that occur. Later you will be asked to take an overview of the way Faulks has used this motif throughout the novel.

Focus on: sense of place

CONSIDER THE USE OF IRONY THROUGH A CLOSE READING . . .

— The Somme is now remembered principally as the setting of the disastrous Allied offensive of 1916. In 1910 it was innocent of that association. Consider how the Somme area is depicted in this scene. Which details anticipate images that have since become motifs of the First World War? What is the effect of the irony that we, as readers, know more than the characters about what is to come?

PART ONE
SECTION 6 (pp. 48–62)

Focus on: the theme of passion and self-control

ANALYSE WITH A CLOSE READING . . .

— Examine how the theme of passion and self-control is developed in this section, on both private and public levels.

— Stephen mused during the picnic excursion that 'the sensation of desire seemed indistinguishable from an impulse towards death' (p. 45). Analyse the language used in the account of Stephen and Isabelle's love-making. What associations are suggested linguistically between their passion, and images of violence, death and oblivion?

COMPARE AND EVALUATE . . .

— Look again at the description of Isabelle's sexual life with Azaire on p. 39: 'she could not understand why this aspect of their lives, which seemed to mean so much to him, was something he would not talk about, nor why the startling intimacy of the act opened no doors in her mind, made no connections with the deeper feelings and aspirations that had grown in her since childhood'. Compare it with this description of sexual intimacy with Stephen on p. 60: 'I am at last what I am, she thought; I was born for this. Fragments of childish longings, of afternoon urges suppressed in the routine of her parents' house, flashed across her mind; she felt at last connections forged between the rage of her desire and a particular attentive recognition of herself, the little Fourmentier girl.' Does the different nature of her sexual experiences with the two men suggest that they have different value?

Focus on: narrative viewpoint

CONSIDER SHIFTS IN VIEWPOINT . . .

— When Stephen and Isabelle move to the red room to make love, the narrative viewpoint moves from his to hers. What is the effect of this shift in perspective?

PART ONE
SECTION 7 (pp. 63–78)

Focus on: characterisation

COMPARE POINTS OF VIEW . . .

— Compare and contrast the ways in which Isabelle and Stephen react to 'what had occurred between them' (p. 67).

Focus on: the theme of love and trust

COMPARE TWO PRESENTATIONS OF LOVE IN ADVERSITY . . .

— The theme of a love that flourishes secretly in a hostile environment is common in literature. The most famous example is probably Shakespeare's play *Romeo and Juliet*. In both cases, the reader's/audience's sympathies are with the lovers, whose families seem somehow at fault. The fact that their love is forbidden gives it an intensity that supports them against adversity, but it also leaves them doubly vulnerable to lovers' insecurities: if the lover proves false, who will offer support? Read Act II, scene 2 of *Romeo and Juliet* – usually referred to as the 'balcony scene' – and compare this lyrical, sixteenth-century portrayal of lovers' declarations with Faulks's twentieth-century prose portrayal. Do the characters' actions have anything in common?

CONSIDER WORDS IN CONTEXTS . . .

— 'adultery' (p. 66). Why is this word so powerful? Compare the connotations of 'love', 'passion', 'infidelity' and 'adultery' as they are commonly used nowadays. Which of these four words would you pick as the most accurate description of the liaison between Stephen and Isabelle, and why?

— 'Save me' (p. 72). What does Stephen mean by 'save' here? What is 'salvation' in Christian theology? Later, you will be asked to consider how the notion of salvation is developed in Part Two of the novel.

— 'a good wife' (p. 76). What does Azaire appear to mean by this expression? What judgements about women's roles are betrayed by it? Which of these judgements reflect the place and the time, and which still exist in your society today?

PART ONE
SECTION 8 (pp. 79–88)

Focus on: sense of place

CONSIDER THE USE OF PLACE-NAMES . . .

— The places that the fishing party passes through on the way to the Ancre (p. 83) were later the sites of significant battles. What is the effect of mentioning such notable place-names of the war in this pre-war context? Compare this effect with that created by the description of the Somme in section 5 (pp. 34–47).

PART ONE
SECTION 9 (pp. 89–108)

Focus on: themes

ANALYSE STORYTELLING . . .

— When Stephen says to Isabelle, 'You will leave the husband who beats you and go with the man who loves you' (p. 91), he is telling a story – the story he hopes they will now play out. This section contains several other instances of characters turning life into narrative. Analyse the ways in which characters put a value on events by telling them as a story. Stephen puts his hopes into words, but Isabelle resists doing so. Why is this?

COMPARE REFERENCES TO TIME . . .

— The theme of the effects of time: read the paragraph on p. 101 beginning 'She dreamed of pale faces . . .' Now turn back to p. 72 and read the two paragraphs from 'So many dead . . .' to '. . . the weight of time'. What point is being made about the 'repeated loop of time'? In what ways does the novel so far seem to present time as destructive of the 'meaning' that people put on their feelings and actions? Later in the novel time will offer new perspectives and new possible meanings to events that seemed meaningless to those who were a part of them.

PART ONE
SECTION 10 (pp. 109–17)

Focus on: themes

COMPARE POINTS OF VIEW . . .

— The theme of religious faith: compare Isabelle's visit to a church on pp. 113–4 with Stephen's visit to a cathedral on pp. 71–2. Consider the ways in which the narrative styles reflect their contrasting ways of thinking. Are there any similarities between their reflections on human attempts to find 'meaning' in life?

CONSIDER MOTIVATION . . .
— The theme of trust and betrayal: why does Isabelle keep her pregnancy secret from Stephen? What impulses drive her to leave him? Are we told anything about her character (here or earlier) that might explain her motivation?

DISCUSS . . .
— The theme of body and spirit: Isabelle thinks of Christ's suffering, and muses on how it is difficult to see the human experience as anything beyond physical experience. Are there any indications that her love for Stephen was more than merely physical? And his love for her? What do you think? Do you believe that human experience is confined to our physical existence, or do you think that human beings have a soul that outlives the body? What are the 'highest' human values and ideals? These questions will become increasingly central to the novel's themes.

PART ONE

Looking over Part One

QUESTIONS FOR DISCUSSION OR ESSAYS
1. Consider the ways in which victory and defeat are explored on a personal level in Part One.

2. Writers have often depicted the period before the start of the First World War nostalgically, as a serene and golden time. But Faulks combines nostalgia with a less serene picture. In

what ways has he highlighted tensions within French society of the period?

3. What kinds of significance does the motif of birdsong take on in Part One?

4. How does Faulks employ a sense of place in Part One?

5. Consider the presentation of passion in Part One.

6. Stephen later says of his behaviour in Part One, 'I was rash and curious and selfish' (p. 472). Assess the validity of this claim.

7. 'Part One presents characters as pitiful, driven by passions they cannot control in a world they cannot understand.' Discuss.

8. Consider the significance of 'home' in Part One.

9. Discuss the themes of boundaries, trespasses and guilt in Part One.

PART TWO. FRANCE, 1916.

Focus on: historical background

RESEARCH . . .
— In what ways did the war of 1914–18 become markedly different from any other war that had gone before?
— In what ways is 1916 now regarded as a turning point in the First World War?

PART TWO
SECTIONS I AND 2 (pp. 121–38)

Focus on: sense of place

ANALYSE WITH A CLOSE READING . . .

— Still in France, but two years into the war, the characters seem to inhabit another world from that of Part One. Pick out ten details in pp. 121–38 that convey the world Jack Firebrace now inhabits, his role in it and his reactions to the events of this section. How are details of his life back in England used to create contrasts with his experiences of war?

Focus on: letters as a narrative technique

CONSIDER COMMUNICATION BY LETTER . . .

— Margaret's letter to Jack is the fourth letter in the novel so far. The first three were Stephen's unsent letter to his employer (pp. 52–3), Marguerite's letter to Isabelle (p. 106) and Isabelle's letter to Jeanne (pp. 114–15). One might include as a fifth the letter that Isabelle did not write to Stephen after leaving him. Pick any one of these letters and consider what it says and what it does not say. In what ways is communication by letter different from communication by speech? What things are easier to say by letter than in speech, and what things are harder?

— Margaret writes to Jack Firebrace about their son, John. Isabelle does not write to Stephen about their daughter. What is the effect of this contrast?

Focus on: the theme of salvation

COMPARE BY A CLOSE READING . . .

— Jack Firebrace 'held his head in his hands and prayed to God to save him' (p. 131). Look back to p. 72, when Stephen prays 'Save me'. What does 'save' mean in each of these instances?

Focus on: courts martial

RESEARCH THE HISTORICAL BACKGROUND . . .

— 'If he was found guilty by court martial he could be shot' (p. 130). The number of men in the British Army who were summarily executed by firing squads after conviction by courts martial for cowardice, neglect of duty or desertion was officially 346. It has been suggested that many of these men were treated with great injustice for the sake of example: they were often tried by junior officers, inadequately defended, told of their impending deaths only the evening before or that same morning, and denied the right of appeal. To understand more about the circumstances of their deaths, refer to Anthony Babington's *For the Sake of Example, Capital Courts Martial 1914–18: the Truth* (1983). Or look up newspaper articles on the question of whether executed soldiers should be pardoned, such as those in *The Times* of 25 July 1998 or 6 November 1998.

Focus on: characterisation

RELATE TWO POINTS OF VIEW . . .

— Stephen enters the novel again, seen from Jack Firebrace's point of view. What aspects of Stephen are emphasised in this description, and in what ways is this a new perspective on his character? Which differences might be the result of the time that has passed since Part One, and which might be coloured by Jack's point of view?

PART TWO
SECTIONS 3 and 4 (pp. 139–56)

*Focus on: the theme of the boundaries
of human behaviour*

DISCUSS . . .

— 'None of these men would admit that what they saw and what they did were beyond the boundaries of human behaviour' (p. 141). How many instances of actions that are 'beyond the boundaries of human behaviour' have you found in Part Two so far? Make a list of ten such actions that are committed in wartime, and discuss why, in your opinion, these actions might be beyond such 'boundaries'.

COMPARE WITH A CLOSE READING TWO
PRESENTATIONS OF WAR . . .

— Read the paragraph beginning 'All right. I'll tell you something' on p. 150, in which Stephen says men will always 'do more', no matter how degrading (and note that this is another story by which he makes sense of his experiences). Now read Henry V's rallying speech beginning 'Once more unto the breach, dear friends, once more' in Act III, scene 1 of Shakespeare's *Henry V*. Contrast Stephen's and Henry's images of war and its significance.

Focus on: characterisation

ANALYSE AND COMPARE . . .

— Stephen is six years older than he was in Part One, and so far in Part Two we have only seen him from other people's points of view. From p. 145 onwards the narrative reverts to his point of view, and we see how he thinks. In what ways has his character developed since Part One, and in what ways is it similar?

Focus on: the theme of the dehumanising effects of war

EXAMINE . . .

— 'They were men who could each have a history but, in the shadow of what awaited them, were interchangeable' (p. 144). Explore how these sections of the novel have emphasised the dehumanising effect of the men's military roles.

PART TWO
SECTIONS 5 and 6 (pp. 157–78)

Focus on: characterisation

ANALYSE AND RELATE . . .

— In these sections we see some of the complexity lying behind Stephen's 'coldness'. What do we learn? What new light does this throw on his actions up to this point in the novel?

Focus on: the theme of instinct and self-control

REFLECT AND PRESENT . . .

— The scenes in the tunnel emphasise the characters' fear of confined space and of the weight of earth on top of them. Stephen controls his fear by focusing on his hatred of the Germans. Have you ever been in a situation in which you had to fight panic? What was the situation? Did you manage to control your panic, and if so, how?

PART TWO
SECTIONS 7 and 8 (pp. 179–84)

Focus on: *characterisation*

ASSESS A CHARACTER'S BELIEFS . . .
— Stephen believes that the men do not respect him, and that he has never been loved. Assess whether he is right. Consider in particular Firebrace's and Weir's attitudes towards Stephen in these two sections.

PART TWO
SECTION 9 (pp. 185–93)

Focus on: *the theme of human pity*

COMPARE PRESENTATIONS OF SUFFERING IN POETRY AND PROSE . . .
— Wilfred Owen's poetry concentrates on the physical and mental destruction caused by war. 'My subject is War, and the pity of War. The poetry is in the pity,' he wrote. Read his poems 'Dulce et Decorum Est' and 'Disabled'. Compare the effect of these poems with the effects created by Faulks in this section in his description of the boy's pain and death and of the nurse's attempts to help him.

ANALYSE AND DISCUSS . . .
— 'Compassion has more value than passion.' Discuss, with reference to Stephen's experiences in Parts One and Two of *Birdsong*.

PART TWO
SECTION 10 (pp. 194–207)

Focus on: the theme of love

COMPARE . . .
— Following the portrayal of the nurse's compassion, this section shows Weir, Stephen and Firebrace contemplating two more kinds of love: erotic love and paternal love. Compare the presentation of these three types of love in the novel so far.

Focus on: the theme of the boundaries of human behaviour

INTERPRET AND DISCUSS . . .
— Why does Stephen react as he does to the younger prostitute? Do you consider any of Stephen's actions in this passage to be 'beyond the boundaries of human behaviour' (cf. p. 141)?

PART TWO
SECTION 11 (pp. 208–12)

Focus on: characterisation

IMAGINE . . .
— Margaret's letter is very dignified and controlled, and suggests that, for Jack's sake, she has hidden the extent of her own suffering. Imagine that you are Margaret. Write your thoughts about John and about your husband at this point in the novel.

47

PART TWO
SECTION 12 (pp. 213–37)

Focus on: narrative technique

ANALYSE WITH A CLOSE READING . . .
— In what ways does the narrative create a sense of fore-boding in this section? How does Faulks play on the irony that the reader probably knows that the Allies suffered devastating losses in the Somme offensive?

COMPARE TWO PRESENTATIONS OF APPREHENSION . . .
— What is the effect of the letters? Read the poem 'Before Action' by W.N. Hodgson, which he wrote two days before his death on 1 July 1916. Compare Hodgson's sentiments with those expressed in the letters in this section.

COMPARE FICTIONAL AND FIRST-HAND ACCOUNTS OF BATTLE . . .
— Read the chapter entitled 'Battle' in Denis Winter's *Death's Men, Soldiers of the Great War* (1979) for first-hand accounts of what it is like to go into battle. Compare these with Faulks's account in this section. What similarities and differences can you find between this 'fictional' and those first-hand accounts?

Focus on: the theme of love

COMPARE CHARACTERS' ATTITUDES . . .
— Stephen told Weir that he never thought about Isabelle any more. Later he thinks that she never loved him, that she aban-doned him, and that he cannot forgive her. Given all of this, why does Stephen write to her? What need in him does evoking her spirit help to meet? Contrast Stephen's neediness with Jack Firebrace's attitude to his wife in his letter.

Focus on: the Somme, 1916

The first day of the battle of the Somme has become a defining moment of the war in modern memory, a moment that symbolises the waste of young lives and marks a growing disillusionment among soldiers with the way the war was being fought. See the author interview for Faulks's comments about how the First World War redrew our attitudes and expectations about war and authority.

RESEARCH THE HISTORICAL BACKGROUND . . .
— Read the short chapter 'The Face of Battle – The Somme 1916' in Malcolm Brown's *Tommy Goes to War* (1978) for some historical background, including photographs.

COMPARE FICTIONAL AND HISTORICAL ACCOUNTS . . .
— Read an account of this day from a historical source and compare it with this section of the novel. By describing the first day of the Somme from Stephen's point of view, Faulks conveys what it might have been like to experience the battle 'on the ground'. Which aspects of battle does Faulks's fictional narrative emphasise differently from the historical account?

Focus on: themes

RELATE THEMATIC IDEAS TO THE NARRATIVE . . .
— Discuss how the following statements are dramatised in the novel:

- 'Nothing was divine any more; everything was profane' (p. 230).
- 'Stephen watched the packets of lives with their memories and loves go spinning and vomiting to the ground' (p. 232).
- 'It was not the tens of thousands of deaths that mattered;

49

it was the way they had proved that you could be human yet act in a way that was beyond nature' (p. 234).

COMPARE AND DISCUSS VIEWPOINTS . . .

— Stephen finds himself jostling with German soldiers in the river. 'Close to, in their pitted skin and wide eyes, he saw men like himself' (p. 234). The hatred he has cultivated against the Germans falters at this proximity; without the boundary of no-man's-land to separate them from him, he is reminded of their shared humanity. Why do we not usually read German poetry of the First World War? Look up and read some poems by German soldiers (such as 'Clearing Station' by Wilhelm Klemm). Or read the chapter 'Humanity and Hatred' in Malcolm Brown's *The Imperial War Museum Book of the First World War* (1991). Discuss your reactions to reading these texts.

— Faulks comments in the author interview that one of the questions that fascinated him was why no one involved in the Somme offensive – neither the Allied soldiers who were advancing, nor the German soldiers who were killing them – simply said, 'I can't do this.' Discuss why. For a fuller understanding, read Chapter 12, 'Why men fought', in Niall Ferguson's *The Pity of War* (1998).

Focus on: historical perspective

DISCUSS THE REPERCUSSIONS NOW OF EVENTS THEN . . .

— Of the 800 men in Stephen's battalion, 155 return. This number gives local shape to the massive figures of history, which tell us that some 60,000 Allied lives were lost on the first day of the Somme alone (in contrast to 8,000 German casualties). In total, the British suffered some 420,000 losses in the Somme offensive and the French some 205,000. Germany put her official losses at 450,000, although the British estimated them as being much higher. Think about these numbers: how many lives were touched by these deaths? Discuss the ways in which these deaths still have repercussions today.

PART TWO
SECTION 13 (pp. 238–40)

Focus on: narrative shape

RELATE A PART TO THE WHOLE . . .
— What does this brief section add to the novel?

Focus on: the theme of faith

EXPLAIN . . .
— Stephen tells Weir to 'Hold on'. To what?

PART TWO

Looking over Part Two

QUESTIONS FOR DISCUSSION OR ESSAYS
1.   Does Part Two of *Birdsong* suggest that war has a moral code of its own?

2.   Stephen is referred to as 'cold' several times at the start of Part Two, but then these references stop. Discuss the ways in which his experiences of war have changed Stephen by the end of the second part.

3.   Consider the contribution to Part Two made by two or more of the following characters: Shaw, Gray, Byrne, Weir.

4. Compare the ways in which the theme of boundaries is developed in Parts One and Two of *Birdsong*.

5. Discuss the theme of nature's indifference in Part Two.

6. 'Hardly one soldier in a hundred was inspired by religious feeling of even the crudest kind' (Graves). Discuss Faulks's presentation of faith in the second part of *Birdsong*.

7. 'War drives home the truth that, whatever else human beings are, whatever their hopes and feelings, their personalities and memories, in the end they are little more than flesh and blood.' Discuss Faulks's presentation of war in the light of this comment.

8. Compare the presentation of love in Parts One and Two.

9. Contrast the ways in which the theme of private conscience and public role is developed in Parts One and Two of *Birdsong*.

LONGER COMPARATIVE AND CONTEXTUAL QUESTIONS

1. Is war ever justifiable? Research the notion of a 'just war' in a dictionary of ideas or an encyclopaedia. In discussing conduct in war that is 'justified', Thomas Aquinas focused on the idea of *proportionality* – that the use of violence be commensurate with the purposes of the war. Did the First World War violate this principle? Read Robert Graves's account of atrocities in *Goodbye to All That* (1929), pp. 153–5 in the Penguin edition. Some later writers have questioned Graves's veracity. The question continually presents itself: who is to be believed?

2. Compare Faulks's fictional presentation of the soldiers' experience of trench warfare with that in another genre or medium, such as the displays at London's Imperial War Museum,

a television documentary, a film narrative. Is Faulks's account true to life? What elements has he altered or omitted?

3. Look up 'tragedy' in the glossary of literary terms. Read Shakespeare's tragedy *King Lear*. In the early 1600s, when Shakespeare wrote *King Lear*, tragedies were always about people of high social rank. During the twentieth century ordinary people with ordinary strengths and weaknesses became frequent subjects of 'tragic' literature (see, for instance, the significantly named Willy Loman of Arthur Miller's *Death of a Salesman*). Compare Lear's loss of his daughter Cordelia in Act V of that play with Jack Firebrace's loss of his son on pp. 208–12. Can Firebrace's suffering be called 'tragic'? What techniques have been used in each instance to emphasise the apparent injustice and inexplicable nature of human suffering?

4. The songs of various birds, such as swallows, doves, larks, a blackbird, thrushes, rooks and a nightingale, have formed a backdrop to events so far in the novel. Many poems, letters and memoirs mention the surprise that birdsong could bring to soldiers – a reminder that nature continued, indifferent to their situation. Some poetry gave birdsong symbolic overtones. Read 'Returning, we hear the Larks' by Isaac Rosenberg, and 'Magpies in Picardy' by T.P. Cameron Wilson. What connotations does the birdsong have for the speaker of each poem? Research the symbolic connotations of the nightingale and its song. Read the classical tale of Philomela. Or read Keats's 'Ode to a Nightingale' (1819), in which he uses a number of traditional symbolic values of the nightingale's song: it is an equivalent for human song, for poetry and for an imagined world of ideal beauty, which the poem contrasts with the real world of suffering and death. Is Faulks using any of these traditional symbols in his reference to the nightingale on p. 197? What use has he made of traditional literary images of birdsong in this novel so far?

5. Edward Thomas's poem 'Adlestrop' was written during the First World War, but it is set in England. Compare his use of the image of birdsong with that employed by Faulks in the novel as a whole.

PART THREE. ENGLAND, 1978.
SECTION 1 (pp. 243–50)

The milieu of near-contemporary London is as immediately familiar to most readers as that of 1916 France was unfamiliar. The two worlds are far apart in time and in atmosphere, but they are bound by innumerable connections. Some of these are suggested aesthetically by echoes of images or themes, and some are uncovered in the narrative. One of the themes of Part Three is the modern world's ignorance of its debt to the past.

COMPARE WITH CLOSE ATTENTION TO WORD
CHOICE . . .
— Stephen 'had become, in some way he did not understand, wedded to [the war]: his small destiny was tied to the larger outcome of events' (p. 190). 'But something about the war had unsettled [Elizabeth]: it seemed to touch an area of disquiet and curiosity that was connected to her own life and its choices' (p. 250). Although these two statements express similar ideas, the language each uses is tellingly different. Analyse the significance of 'wedded' and 'tied' compared with 'connected'; of 'his small destiny' compared with 'her own life and its choices'; and consider the impact of the word 'disquiet' in comparison with sounds of war and of birdsong.

Focus on: characterisation

SUMMARISE AND ANALYSE . . .
— This section introduces the character of Elizabeth Benson. What do we learn about her — her life, her personality, her values — and how is this information conveyed?

RESEARCH AND PRESENT . . .
— Elizabeth wants to track down her grandfather in order to understand herself. In what respects are we defined by our forebears? Research the lives of one of your grandparents — perhaps the one you know least about. Does it throw any light on your own life, on your personality, on the way your parents have brought you up? If you are working with a group or a class, give a five-minute presentation to them about what you have discovered.

PART THREE
SECTION 2 (pp. 251–7)

Focus on: social mores

COMPARE PAST AND PRESENT SOCIAL CONTEXTS . . .
— Examine the circumstances of Elizabeth's life compared with those of Isabelle in Part One. Can you find any similarities in disposition, taste or outlook? Which contrasts in the circumstances of their lives are due to the different social expectations of women that existed in Amiens in 1910 and in London in 1978?

DISCUSS THE SIGNIFICANCE OF THE PAST . . .
— Erich and Irene know little about the First World War, and are not very interested in finding out. Does it matter that people

alive today should know what happened? If so, why? Or is the past best forgotten? Discuss these questions with your group, if you are in one.

PART THREE
SECTION 3 (pp. 258–62)

Focus on: sense of place

COMPARE IMAGES OF LOST WORLDS . . .
— Contrast the impression portrayed of Arras in 1978 with the descriptions of French local areas in 1910 in Part One. What, by implication, has been lost in the intervening sixty-eight years? Now read the poem 'MCXIV' by Philip Larkin, in which he attempts to capture the mood of England in 1914, at the outset of the First World War. How does he create the atmosphere of pre-war England in this poem? What aspects suggest a world now lost?

PART THREE
SECTION 4 (pp. 263–4)

Focus on: memorials

ANALYSE . . .
— Reread the description of the memorial to the 'lost' that Elizabeth discovers, and analyse the developing stages of her reactions to it.

Focus on: the theme of loss and being lost

CONSIDER THE VARIANT MEANINGS OF 'LOST' . . .

— What connotations does the word 'lost' (p. 264) have? Consider what is 'lost' by characters in Parts One and Two of *Birdsong*. In which ways are characters themselves 'lost'? In some senses the society they lost their lives for is not the society in which we now live. What has been lost, and what has been gained, in return for their sacrifice?

PART THREE
SECTIONS 5 and 6 (pp. 265–78)

Focus on: the past as against the present

LOOK AT THE TOPOGRAPHY . . .

— Elizabeth arrives on the Continent at Calais and drives to Brussels. Look at the area she drives through on the map. Within the context of *Birdsong*, what is the significance of the route of the journey that she makes, and the fact that she makes it so easily?

Focus on: war as 'sacrifice'

LOOK UP THE WORD 'SACRIFICE' . . .

— 'it was difficult to see her own life as the pinnacle of previous generations' sacrifices' (p. 271). What does 'sacrifice' mean? Is it accurate to apply this word to the deaths of soldiers in the First World War, or is such usage a euphemism for 'waste'?

Focus on: time

COMPARE DIFFERENT DEPICTIONS OF TIME'S EFFECTS . . .

— When Elizabeth looks at Stephen's papers, we see the events of his life that were earlier described as living now exist only as dry, dusty papers that Françoise did not value enough to preserve. Read Philip Larkin's 'Love Songs in Age', or (if you have more time) Keats's poem 'The Eve of St Agnes', which places the story of a passionate and sensual love affair within the framework of time that robs life of its richness. Compare the way in which either of these poems presents time's effects with the way *Birdsong* presents them.

ANALYSE WITH A CLOSE READING . . .
— It is confirmed in this section that Stephen is Elizabeth's grandfather. What suggestions are there that Elizabeth is also related to Isabelle? Consider her temperament as well as circumstantial hints. These unconfirmed suggestions intimate that perhaps Elizabeth owes her life to Stephen and Isabelle's affair. What new perspectives would this put on the events of Part One?

PART THREE

Looking over Part Three

QUESTIONS FOR DISCUSSION OR ESSAYS
1. How does Part Three play on the irony that the reader knows more about Stephen's life than his granddaughter does, and can see connections that she is unaware of?

2. Compare and contrast Elizabeth's character with Isabelle's.

3. Compare and contrast the role of women in contemporary London with their role in Amiens at the start of the century, as both are depicted in *Birdsong*.

4. 'The differences in the love affairs between Stephen and Isabelle in 1910 and between Elizabeth and Robert in 1978 foreground the contrasting mores of these two periods.' Discuss.

5. Find patterned images in Part Three of *Birdsong* that suggest connections between the past and the present.

6. Discuss the significance of remembering in Part Three of *Birdsong*.

7. The final lines of Shakespeare's *King Lear* are 'we that are young/Shall never see so much, nor live so long'. Consider the claim that in Part Three of *Birdsong* Faulks presents the younger generation as ignorant and unwise compared to their grandparents' generation.

PART FOUR. FRANCE, 1917.
SECTION 1 (pp. 281–9)

Focus on: home

ANALYSE . . .
— Weir told Stephen on p. 153 that he joined the army to get away from home. After two years at war he needed to feel 'at home', 'restored to his old sense of self' on home leave, but the experience disappoints: he no longer belongs. Analyse the miscommunication between Weir and his parents.

PART FOUR
SECTION 2 (pp. 290–8)

Focus on: faith

REFLECT AND DISCUSS . . .
— What is the appeal of magic? Explaining the inexplicable? Occupying the region of hope, in place of love and caring? Providing a make-believe world for people who cannot believe in the real one? Discuss Stephen's attitude towards magic in this section.

INTERPRET . . .
— What is Stephen's attitude towards Weir? He later explains (p. 309) why he does the cards for Weir: because Weir 'doesn't believe in anything'. Stephen said earlier (p. 164), 'I don't know what anything is worth', but he now seems to have found faith in something. Interpret what he means about this on p. 296.

OUTLINE . . .
— Describe the various ways in which the characters try to find meaning against the odds, in this section and in Part Two.

PART FOUR
SECTION 3 (pp. 299–307)

Focus on: symbols

ACCOUNT FOR . . .
— Given the brutality of their war experiences, account for the fact that neither man can kill the canary. What does the bird symbolise to Stephen?

PART FOUR
SECTION 4 (pp. 308–23)

Focus on: the theme of fear

DEFINE . . .

— When talking with Ellis, Stephen distinguishes between the fear of physical danger and Weir's fear that the war has 'no purpose'. Define as accurately as you can the differences between these two fears.

Focus on: characterisation

ANALYSE AND COMPARE . . .

— Explore Stephen's reaction to meeting Jeanne. What seem to be his feelings towards Isabelle at this point? Bear in mind his earlier letter to Isabelle (p. 222). Compare your ideas with what we are told in the next section.

— Compare the scene of Stephen's conversation with Jeanne with his earlier conversation with Isabelle on pp. 28–30. In what ways is he opportunistic in both? Look carefully at what Jeanne says. Which are the key words that she uses? Analyse what they reveal of her character.

PART FOUR
SECTION 5 (pp. 324–36)

Focus on: narrative point of view

ANALYSE THE EFFECTS OF THE NARRATIVE TECHNIQUE . . .

— Look at how Faulks handles the narrative point of view in this section. The reader knows more about Isabelle than Stephen does (about her child, for instance), but here Faulks delays the revelation of whatever it is Jeanne is withholding until Stephen himself realises it. What effects are created by telling these events from Stephen's point of view? Later the point of view moves from Stephen's to Isabelle's. At what moment does this happen? What is the effect of this change?

Focus on: characterisation

INTERPRET . . .
— Why is Isabelle's scar so shocking to Stephen?

COMPARE CHARACTERS . . .
— In Part One, Stephen was implicitly contrasted with Azaire: the contrast worked in Stephen's favour. Now he is implicitly contrasted with Max. In what ways does this contrast throw into relief some of Stephen's flaws?

CONSIDER MAX AND ISABELLE . . .
— How does the story of Max's devotion to Isabelle and to Stephen's child alter our perception of the information that Max and Stephen are enemies on the same part of the Somme?
— 'This was her final chance to redeem herself . . . The more difficult it became, the more important they both knew that it was for them to honour the pledges they had made to each other' (p. 334). In what ways is Isabelle 'redeeming' herself through her devotion to Max?
— Consider the ways in which Faulks enlists our sympathies for Isabelle in this section.

PART FOUR
SECTION 6 (pp. 337–41)

Focus on: intimacy

COMPARE DIFFERENT FORMS OF INTIMACY . . .
— Contrast the nature of the intimacy of Stephen touching Isabelle's scar on p. 336 with the 'intimate moment' Stephen recalls with Gray on p. 341. To what extent do the characters involved seek intimacy?

PART FOUR
SECTION 7 (pp. 342–47)

Focus on: the theme of loss

DISCUSS . . .
— By relating this section to the whole, discuss how the novel conveys the brutalising effects of too much loss.

Focus on: song

RESEARCH . . .
— Look up the lyrics to popular songs of the First World War, such as 'Pack up your Troubles', 'It's a long way to Tipperary' and 'If you were the only girl in the world'. What attitudes to war and to home do these songs convey?

JUXTAPOSE . . .
— '"Pack up your Troubles" and all that stuff?' said Irene (on p. 256). 'Terrible business, wasn't it?' Compare this facile comment with the account of Jack Firebrace smothering his unbearable grief at losing Shaw by singing. What does this

juxtaposition imply about a contemporary understanding of the First World War?

Focus on: love

DISCUSS . . .
— Jack Firebrace thinks: 'I have made this mistake in my life . . . not once but twice I have loved someone more than my heart would bear' (p. 345). Discuss whether you think this was a mistake.

PART FOUR
SECTION 8 (pp. 348–52)

Focus on: men as flesh

EXPLAIN YOUR REACTIONS . . .
— The description of the men retrieving bodies that are rotting, with images of human beings reduced to rat meat, is shocking. (You might compare this description with some of Siegfried Sassoon's more explicit poems, like 'Counter-Attack'.) How do you react to such visually explicit images? Are they obscene, or are they justified by their artistic purpose in the narrative?

INTERPRET . . .
— 'All night he sang for his brother, whom he had brought home in his hands.' Why was it so important to Brennan that his brother's body should be found, brought back from no-man's-land and buried, do you think?

PART FOUR
SECTION 9 (pp. 353–64)

Focus on: compassion

DEFINE . . .

— Jeanne's primary quality is her 'compassion'. What does this word mean? Look it up in a dictionary. Now look back at her conversations with Stephen on pp. 320–3 and pp. 326–7. Can you find evidence of compassion here? Why is it such an attractive quality to Stephen?

Focus on: 'home'

REFLECT AND EXPLAIN . . .

— This is the first time we have seen Stephen in England, and it is clear that he does not feel 'at home' there. Does the attitude of the civilians surprise you? Can you account for it?

Focus on: the theme of redemption

ANALYSE WITH A CLOSE READING . . .

— The final paragraphs, from 'The hedgerows were deep . . .' (p. 362) to the end of the section, combine the language of literary pastoral with the language of Christian theology. The novel has seemed to stress nature's indifference until this point. Now Stephen is overcome by 'a passionate affinity' with nature, 'the force of a binding love'. Look carefully at how this passage combines pastoral and Christian language and analyse the nature of the 'redemption' that Stephen glimpses.

PART FOUR
SECTION 10 (pp. 365–70)

Focus on: characterisation

ANALYSE AND SUM UP . . .
— What qualities does Jeanne embody in this section?
— What impressions have you formed of Jeanne and Isabelle's father, both in this section and earlier (e.g. pp. 330–1)?

PART FOUR
SECTION 11 (pp. 371–81)

Focus on: the satire of military planning

ANALYSE SATIRICAL EFFECT . . .
— Which words in the opening paragraphs on p. 371 suggest a satirical view of military planning, both by the narrator and by Stephen and Gray? What is the ironic effect of the statement that Jack Firebrace remembered 'how he had prayed for the men who would go over that summer morning and how he had trusted in their safekeeping', coming so soon afterwards?

Focus on: Stephen and Weir

MAKE INFERENCES . . .
— What is Weir trying to say to Stephen on pp. 373–4? Why does Stephen not want to hear it?

Focus on: going over

COMPARE FICTIONAL AND FIRST-HAND ACCOUNTS . . .
— Is it possible to imagine what it is like to go over the top if one has never done it? Compare this passage with accounts

by men who went through this experience. Look, for instance, at the chapter 'Zero Hour and After: The Experience of Battle' in Malcolm Brown's *The Imperial War Museum Book of the First World War* (1991). Compare and contrast these accounts of real experience with the novel's fictional account.

Focus on: Stephen

ASSESS STEPHEN'S DEVELOPMENT . . .
— 'Stephen watched their foolish, crab-like movements and felt his heart seize up with pitying love for them' (p. 376). In what ways has Stephen changed since the start of the novel?
— Why does Stephen stick to orders? Was he right to do so?

PART FOUR
SECTION 12 (pp. 382–3)

Focus on: letters of condolence

IMAGINE . . .
— Do you imagine that Mrs Ellis would find this letter consoling? What do you imagine she would have liked to hear?

PART FOUR
SECTION 13 (pp. 384–90)

Focus on: Weir's death

ANALYSE STYLE . . .
— What is the effect of the matter-of-fact way in which Weir's death is described?

DISCUSS . . .
— 'Weir alone had made the war bearable,' thinks Stephen (p. 385). Discuss the friendship between Stephen and Weir.

COMPARE CHARACTERS' RESPONSES . . .
— Contrast Stephen's response to Weir's death with Jack Firebrace's response to Shaw's death on p. 345. What is the nature of the 'love' that Stephen and Jack felt for the two dead men?

Focus on: intelligence-gathering

PLACE AN EPISODE IN CONTEXT . . .
— What do you think is the point of the intelligence-gathering episode? Consider the characterisation of Lallement, and compare what he says with Gray's remarks about French morale immediately before.

Focus on: Stephen's characterisation

ANALYSE NARRATIVE STRUCTURE . . .
— Stephen feels his life is grey and thin, and without meaning. Think of the events of Part Three, set in the 1970s, and consider the effects of Gray's remark 'Then do it for our children' (p. 388). Consider also Jeanne's encouragement, 'Do it for my sake' (p. 390). Is Stephen's life as meaningless as he thinks?

PART FOUR

Looking over Part Four

QUESTIONS FOR DISCUSSION OR ESSAYS
1. Consider the ways in which Stephen's character develops in Part Four.

2. Discuss the theme of redemption in Part Four.

3. Consider the validity of the claim that 'Isabelle's story is a critique of the social inequality of women at the time'.

4. Discuss the themes of intimacy and isolation in the novel so far.

5. 'The difference between life and death was not one of fact but merely of time' (cf. pp. 72, 349). What does this statement mean?

6. In the world of Part Four, where 'random violence . . . ran supreme' (p. 342), how potent is love as a redeeming value?

PART FIVE. ENGLAND, 1978–9.
SECTION I (pp. 393–8)

Focus on: the past and the present

REFLECT AND DISCUSS . . .

— 'People don't always appreciate what sacrifices were made for them.' (p. 393). Look back at Gray's encouragement to Stephen to 'do it for our children' (p. 388). In your opinion, do we appreciate enough the sacrifice that was made for our sake? Or are painful national memories of trauma best forgotten? Read Sassoon's poem 'Aftermath' and discuss whether it is better to remember or to forget the traumas of the First World War.

DRAW LINKS THROUGH WORDS . . .

— Stuart phones for 'a chat'. The word 'chat' originally meant a louse, and 'chatting' was the ritual of delousing verminous shirts using thumbnails and candle flames; eventually it came to mean the conversation that accompanied this ritual. Jack Firebrace recalls 'chatting' for Shaw on pp. 345–6. If Faulks is inviting through this echo a comparison of the heartfelt love of Firebrace for Shaw with the half-hearted flirtation between Stuart and Elizabeth, what is the point of the comparison?

PART FIVE
SECTION 2 (pp. 399–405)

Focus on: *human pity*

COMMENT WITH A CLOSE READING . . .
— Look back to p. 352, the last time that Brennan figured in the novel. Compare the two portrayals of him. How does this section emphasise 'the pity of the past'?

Focus on: *sacrifice*

RELATE THE SECTION TO THE WHOLE . . .
— What does this section add to the novel's themes of sacrifice and the debt owed by the modern world to those who fought in the First World War?

PART FIVE
SECTION 3 (pp. 406–9)

Focus on: *relationships*

COMPARE CHARACTERS' ATTITUDES . . .
— Assess the attitudes of Robert and Elizabeth towards their relationship. Then compare these with Stephen and

Isabelle's attitudes towards their affair in Parts One and Four. Look in particular at their different attitudes towards 'difficult decisions' (e.g. pp. 334 and 409). To what extent are the contrasts down to differences of character, and to what extent are they down to the different social mores of their times?

PART FIVE
SECTION 4 (pp. 410–16)

Focus on: past and present

COMPARE DETAILS . . .
— Look at the details in this section that connect details from Stephen's life, whether literal (the diaries, the buckle), metaphorical (how Elizabeth entertains Stuart compared with how Jeanne provided food and whiskey for Stephen) or symbolic (Stuart's facility with words, compared with Stephen's secretive use of code). What is the effect of these parallels?

Focus on: characterisation

COMPARE CHARACTERS . . .
— Compare and contrast Stuart with Stephen.

PART FIVE
SECTION 5 (pp. 417–22)

Focus on: pregnancy

COMPARE CHARACTERS' ATTITUDES . . .
— Examine Elizabeth's reaction to her pregnancy on p. 419. Compare it with Isabelle's reaction on p. 109. Pick the words that carry the greatest significance and discuss what they reveal.

Focus on: shock

DEFINE . . .
— What does the word 'shock' mean? It is used twice in this section, once each of Elizabeth (p. 417) and Robert (p. 420). Compare their shock with Brennan's 'shellshock' (p. 401) in section 2.

Focus on: telling

RELATE A PART TO THE WHOLE . . .
— Bob cracks Stephen's code, and Elizabeth finally has access to the past and to Stephen's thoughts. This entry contains a hint as to why he has written in code. What do Stephen's diaries add to the theme of 'telling' in the novel?

ANALYSE THE LANGUAGE . . .
— Consider the language used by Stephen in his diary (once decoded). In what ways could it be called anti-rhetorical?

PART FIVE

Looking over Part Five

QUESTIONS FOR DISCUSSION OR ESSAYS

1. Why is Elizabeth so intent on establishing a 'vital connection' with the past?

2. Like Part Three, Part Five implies contrasts between Stephen's world and the modern world. What are the effects of these contrasts?

3. How is the theme of 'the debt we owe' developed in Part Five?

4. Discuss Faulks's presentation of relationships in Part Five.

5. Discuss the theme of communication in Part Five.

6. In what ways do the characters' experiences in the First World War give the lives of contemporary characters 'meaning'?

7. What does Part Five add to the theme of love in the novel?

PART SIX. FRANCE, 1918.
SECTION 1 (pp. 425–7)

Focus on: Stephen

ANALYSE . . .
— The image of Stephen putting away his notebook that comes immediately after the image of Elizabeth reading the

73

same book seems to join the past and the present. Stephen never seems to think of the future, however. What is his state of mind in this section?

PART SIX
SECTION 2 (pp. 428–34)

Focus on: love

COMPARE . . .
— Jeanne tells Stephen 'I love you' (p. 431); eight years earlier Stephen told Isabelle 'I love you' (p. 57) and she said the same (p. 73). Elizabeth has told Robert 'I love you' (p. 420). Compare these four declarations of love. What other kinds of love are there in *Birdsong*?

Focus on: Jeanne

EXAMINE . . .
— We are given a more direct account of Jeanne's thoughts in this section than at any point earlier in the novel. What is her attitude to Stephen here? What human attitudes does she stand for? Using this section as a starting point, examine Jeanne's role in the novel.

PART SIX
SECTION 3 (pp. 435–43)

Focus on: sense of place

ANALYSE . . .
— The setting shifts from the hell of trench warfare to a

different kind of hell underground. Analyse the ways in which Faulks uses physical and symbolic details in these pages to conjure a sense of place in the tunnels. It may help you to refer to entries on the underworld or on caves in a dictionary of Symbolism.

PART SIX
SECTION 4 (pp. 443–50)

Focus on: Stephen

COMPARE . . .

— Stephen first met Jack Firebrace when the latter was up on a charge of falling asleep on sentry duty. Compare Stephen's reactions to Jack Firebrace on that occasion (pp. 133–7) with his reactions to him in this section. Stephen believes (p. 440, 'He watched them depart . . .') that he no longer feels compassion. Does he act compassionately now?

PART SIX
SECTION 5 (pp. 450–6)

Focus on: enforced intimacy

COMMENT . . .

— 'Our own choices may not be so good as those that are made for us,' says Stephen (p. 452). In what ways is it fitting that these two men should have each other for company at what seem to be their last moments?

Focus on: language

COMPARE . . .
— 'There seemed to Stephen something frivolous about their hope . . .' (p. 453). The word 'frivolous' has been used before in the novel: 'Azaire smiled indulgently and shook his head at his wife's frivolous tastes' (pp. 63–4). And 'Elizabeth was struck, not for the first time, by the thought that her life was entirely frivolous' (p. 413). Compare what the word 'frivolous' means in each of these contexts.

Focus on: faith

DISCUSS . . .
— Jack Firebrace thinks of 'the lost illusions of his life . . . The things on which he had based his faith had proved unstable' (p. 454). Using Firebrace as a starting point, discuss the theme of loss of faith in the novel.

PART SIX
SECTION 6 (pp. 456–64)

Focus on: telling details

CONNECT . . .
— Jack Firebrace says that he helped to build the Central Line on London's Underground. When we first see Elizabeth on p. 243 she is travelling on the Central Line. She does not know the connection between her tube journey and her grandfather through Jack Firebrace, of course, but it is there. What is the effect of a small but apparently purposive connection such as this?

Focus on: Stephen

COMMENT ON . . .

— Stephen has been complaining about his 'old good luck, the contemptible voodoo of survival' (p. 442) since Part Two. At the start of this section he thinks 'he would try to sleep and hope not to wake again' (p. 456). But later, 'he worked with a fury given him by hope' (p. 459). Stephen works with extraordinary stamina, 'with the instinct of an animal, brutal, stupid, blind' (p. 462). He wants to die, but he wants to live even more. Comment on the aspects of Stephen's character that come to light in Part Six of *Birdsong*.

Focus on: physicality

ANALYSE WITH A CLOSE READING . . .

— Stephen's situation underground could be read as a metaphor for the general situation of infantry during the First World War One: trapped, forced to live like rats, driven by an animal instinct to survive, despite extraordinary physical hardship. 'Higher' impulses are abandoned and emotions are brutalised. How does Faulks convey the impression of a shrunken world view in which physical matter is all that exists, in this section?

PART SIX
SECTION 7 (pp. 464–9)

Focus on: character sketches

ANALYSE . . .

— Faulks quickly characterises Levi, Kroger and Lamm not as 'the enemy' but as ordinary people. How does he create this impression in these pages?

PART SIX
SECTION 8 (pp. 469–73)

Focus on: the theme of storytelling

ASSESS . . .

— Stephen tells Jack Firebrace 'a story' (p. 472) about his affair with Isabelle. How does he present their love in this story?

PART SIX
SECTION 9 (pp. 473–6)

Focus on: narrative focus

CONSIDER . . .

— Look at how Faulks uses the switch in narrative focus from Stephen to Levi to illustrate Jack Firebrace's claim that 'No one can win' (p. 472).

Focus on: patriotism

DISCUSS . . .

— Levi's reaction to losing his brother is to claim, 'I love the Fatherland . . . A death in my family . . . binds me more than ever to it' (p. 475). That he is Jewish gives this comment an ironic significance. Earlier, to motivate himself to keep going, Stephen says to Jack Firebrace, 'I want to tell you about the Germans and how much I hate them. I'm going to tell you why you've got to live' (p. 471). Discuss the topic 'Patriotism preserves the lie that the enemy are different'.

PART SIX
SECTION 10 (pp. 476–8)

Focus on: Stephen

COMMENT ON . . .
— How do you react to Stephen's words 'I've never had a parcel' (p. 477)? Comment on the light that this detail throws on his character.

Focus on: Jack Firebrace's death

COMPARE . . .
— Examine the low-key way in which Jack Firebrace's death is described (p. 477) and the description of Weir's death (p. 385). What effects are created by the bare style that Faulks uses at these crucial moments?

PART SIX
SECTION 11 (pp. 478–83)

Focus on: revenge and forgiveness

ANALYSE . . .
— Explore what Levi says about why he wants to meet his brother's killer. In this context, what is the significance of Levi being Jewish?
— What impulses drive Stephen and Levi to embrace each other?

PART SIX
SECTION 12 (pp. 484–5)

Focus on: choice of words

CONSIDER . . .
— Think about the effects of the words 'reclaim', 'deliverance' and 'soul' on p. 485.

Focus on: symbols

COMPARE . . .
— Consider the use of symbols of unity in this section: praying together, eating and sleeping together, shaking hands. What is the symbolic significance of the present of the buckle that Levi gives Stephen? You will recall that the buckle has been mentioned before, on p. 412. Reread the conversation about it between Stuart and Elizabeth, which the reader now sees has a proleptic significance. What is the effect of this irony?

Focus on: style

COMPARE . . .
— Contrast the style in which this section is written with the style of pp. 461–4, and account for the different effects which are produced.

Focus on: emotive power

ACCOUNT FOR . . .
— Explain the fact that readers can be moved by the lives of imaginary characters.

PART SIX

Looking over Part Six

QUESTIONS FOR DISCUSSION OR ESSAYS

1. Discuss the contribution made by Jack Firebrace to *Birdsong*.

2. 'Faulks is capable of writing with a wide variety of stylistic effects.' Discuss with reference (not necessarily exclusive) to Part Six.

3. Stephen describes himself ten years earlier as 'rash and curious and selfish' (p. 472). Discuss whether you think he has become less selfish by the end of Part Six.

4. Consider the effects created by the characterisation of Levi in Part Six.

5. Examine the ways in which Part Six forms a conclusion to the parts of the novel set during the First World War.

6. What does Part Six of *Birdsong* contribute to the theme of deliverance in the novel?

PART SEVEN. ENGLAND, 1979.
SECTION 1 (pp. 489–95)

Focus on: eating, drinking, smoking

COMPARE . . .

— The scene in the French restaurant to which Elizabeth and her mother go continues an emphasis on food, wine and cigarettes that has run throughout the novel. The effect here is largely to contrast with the ways in which food, drink and cigarettes were handled during the scenes set in the First World War. Choose an earlier scene (e.g. p. 44, 149, 313–15 or 389) and compare it with this presentation of how characters eat, drink and smoke.

Focus on: narrative strategy

ASSESS THE EFFECT . . .
— The sharp-eyed reader will have noticed hints as early as Part Three that Elizabeth may be Isabelle's granddaughter (an interest in clothes, a liking for jewellery the colour of oxblood, an independent disposition), but confirmation of this link is delayed until now (p. 493). What is the effect of Elizabeth's direct link to Isabelle being confirmed at *this point*?

Focus on: love

DISCUSS . . .
— Françoise's view of love (pp. 494–5) stresses its redemptive value. Does the novel as a whole support this view?

Focus on: Jeanne

DISCUSS . . .
— Françoise says of Jeanne, 'She was the heroine of the whole story' (p. 495). Do you agree?

Focus on: resolution

ANALYSE . . .
— What do you think Elizabeth means when she says that everything is 'all right now' (p. 495)?

PART SEVEN
SECTION 2 (pp. 495–503)

Focus on: themes

COMPARE AND DISCUSS . . .
— Reread pp. 110–15 ('she intended to tell Stephen . . . in this frozen town'), and compare them with pp. 496–8 ('Sometimes she would sit . . . Later, she slept.'). What do these passages contribute to the novel's themes of trust, betrayal, isolation and belonging?

Focus on: intensity

ANALYSE . . .
— Elizabeth earlier complained that, compared with Stephen's generation, her generation had no intensity in their experience (p. 414). In what ways does the description of childbirth show that she is now having an intense experience?

Focus on: hope

COMPARE AND DISCUSS . . .
— When Stephen released Jack Firebrace from the debris of the first explosion, 'he came out like a cork from a bottle, though with a bitter scream' (p. 446). When Robert pulls his child from the womb, 'it suddenly burst free with a sound like a giant cork being released . . . and let out a single bleat' (p. 502). Use this verbal parallel as a starting point for a discussion of the motion: 'The ending of *Birdsong* affirms the victory of life over death, of creation over destruction, and of hope over despair.'

Focus on: imagery

ANALYSE . . .
— What is the effect of the final birdsong of the novel, the 'ambiguous call' of the crow that comes back to earth in 'grating waves' (p. 503)?

COMPARE . . .
— Read Matthew Arnold's poem 'Dover Beach'. Compare what 'Dover Beach' and *Birdsong* say about faith and human suffering.

PART SEVEN

Looking over Part Seven

QUESTION FOR DISCUSSION OR ESSAYS
1. In what ways does Part Seven of *Birdsong* illustrate 'the awkward, compromised and unconquerable existence that made up human life on earth' (p. 178)?

2. Discuss the ways in which Part Seven gives the sense of a completed circle.

3. 'The joyful final images do not reduce the overwhelming sense of the whole: the pity of human experience.' Discuss.

Looking back over the whole novel

QUESTIONS FOR DISCUSSION OR ESSAYS
1. Discuss the variety of forms of love in *Birdsong*.

2. To what effects is the double time-scheme used in the novel?

3.   What does *Birdsong* have to say about attitudes to authority? (You might want to look at what Faulks has to say on this in the interview.)

4.   Discuss Faulks's use of the motif of birdsong in this novel.

5.   Discuss the themes of innocence and guilt in *Birdsong*.

6.   What does *Birdsong* say about faith and despair?

7.   'Despite the characters' failings and weaknesses, the novel asserts a sense of humankind's dignity in their struggle to find meaning in a compromised world.' Discuss.

8.   Discuss the qualities of human nature that offer characters a chance of redemption in *Birdsong*.

9.   What use does Faulks make of letters in *Birdsong*?

10.   '*Birdsong* emphasises the trouble people have in communicating directly and honestly.' Discuss.

11.   Discuss the ways in which characters in *Birdsong* make sense of their experiences by telling stories about them.

12.   'My subject is War, and the pity of War' (Wilfred Owen). Could this statement be accurately applied to *Birdsong*?

13.   Based on your reading of contextual historical material mentioned in these notes, is your impression that Faulks has mythologised the war, or that he has presented events truthfully? (You might want to read Chapter 21, 'The War becomes Myth', in Samuel Hynes's *A War Imagined* [1992]).

14. Does *Birdsong* suggest that the meaning of an event fades with time, or that only after time has passed can its meaning be seen clearly?

15. Why does the First World War have such a power in the modern imagination?

Contexts, comparisons and complementary readings

BIRDSONG

These sections suggest contextual and comparative ways of reading three novels by Faulks. You can put your reading in a social, historical or literary context. You can make comparisons – again, social, literary or historical – with other texts or art works. Or you can choose complementary works (of whatever kind) – that is, art works, literary works, social reportage or facts that in some way illuminate the text by sidelights or interventions which you can make into a telling framework. Some of the suggested contexts are directly connected to the book, in that they give you precise literary or social frames in which to situate the novel. In turn, these are related either to the period within which the novel is set or to the time – now – when you are reading it. Some of these examples are designed to suggest books or other texts that may make useful sources for comparison (or for complementary purposes) when you are reading Faulks's work. Again, they may be related to literary or critical themes, or they may be relevant to social and cultural themes current 'then' or 'now'.

Focus on: the theme of trust and betrayal

ANALYSE AND IMAGINE . . .

— Why is trust so important? Write a pair of short stories: one about trust, the other about betrayal. Try to illustrate why people need to trust, and the way people feel when they are betrayed.

The boundaries of human behaviour

INTERPRET . . .

— As an exercise in the different kinds of boundaries that govern human behaviour, draw three large circles on a sheet of paper so that each circle partly overlaps the other two. One circle is for writing actions that are forbidden because they violate social 'rules' (such as being rude to strangers); the second is for actions that are forbidden by the doctrine of a religion that you practise or know about (such as eating certain kinds of food, or worshipping 'false gods'); the third circle is for actions that you consider beyond natural limits of what is acceptable (such as murder). Now think of at least five actions in each category, and write them in the correct circle. If an action belongs in more than one circle, write it in the shared space. Do any of your chosen actions belong in the space shared by all three circles? Looking at the kinds of things you have written in each circle, which circle contains the most important limits, in your opinion? Now consider how many of the actions you have listed apply equally in wartime, and cross out those that you think do not apply. How different does each of your circles look? Does war alter social rules? Religious rules? Fundamental instincts concerning what is right?

Nature's indifference to human suffering

EVALUATE . . .

— Read the last eleven pages of the chapter entitled 'Trench Life' in Denis Winter's *Death's Men, Soldiers of the Great War* (1979), and discuss the ways in which the natural world seemed indifferent to the experiences of the soldiers.

The First World War in modern memory

SEARCH RESPONSE . . .

— If possible, visit the exhibition on the First World War at the Imperial War Museum in London. When you return, write an essay of one page on the three aspects of the exhibition that surprised you the most. Describe what they were and why they surprised you.

— If you are reading *Birdsong* around the time of early November, watch the Armistice Day ritual on Remembrance Sunday. What is said about the First World War on this occasion? The main purpose of this day is to remember the dead of all the wars in which British and Commonwealth soldiers have fought, but especially those who died in the First World War. What attitude to war do you read in these commemorations?

— Read the chapter 'Persistence and Memory' in Paul Fussell's *The Great War and Modern Memory* (1975).

— What are memorials for, and why are they important? To answer these questions, you could start by reading Chapter 14, 'Monument-Making', in Samuel Hynes's *A War Imagined* (1992). If you can get to London, take a walk from Trafalgar Square to Westminster, studying the statues along the way. Or walk around the part of a town close to you that contains memorials. Pick one memorial that you do not know much about, and research the person or event that it commemorates. Consider the link between history-telling and storytelling in the creation of a nation's identity. Before the fourth plinth in Trafalgar Square (on the far left, as you look at the National Gallery) was set aside for exhibiting art, people debated putting a statue there to commemorate a significant British figure, but there was little agreement about who that person should be. Imagine you have been given the task of commemorating the First World War with a memorial on that plinth. What or who would you commemorate there? Give a brief talk to explain what your choice says about Britain's history.

— Read this advertisement taken from a newspaper in 2001. How does your reading of *Birdsong* help you to account for the continuing interest in the battlefields of the First World War? Would you go on one of these tours?

> The horrors and bravery of the First World War inspired some of our finest soldier poets, including Wilfred Owen, Siegfried Sassoon, Edmund Blunden and Edward Thomas. Holt's tour, *Poetry and Prose of the Great War* (www.battletours.co.uk), follows in their footsteps, looking at the way they recorded their impressions, and showing where they fought and, in some cases, fell. Departing on August 4, the four-day break, led by Barry Webb, biographer of Edmund Blunden – visits Loos, Auchonvilliers, the Oise-Sambre Canal, Arras and Bailleul. The price of £410 covers coach travel from London and half-board hotel accommodation.

— If you can, watch the video of the BBC's 1964 twenty-six-part series on *The Great War*. It is available from the BBC as a five-volume video box and includes documentary footage filmed in the trenches. How do these images of the reality of war compare with the fictional portrayal in Faulks's *Birdsong*?

The influence of history

DISCUSS . . .

— How much do you know about the historical events that shaped the society you live in? Draw up a list of the five historical events that have had most impact on your world today, in order of priority. Then discuss with the rest of the group which five events you have chosen, and why.

The poetry of the First World War

The poetry that came from the experience of the First World War forms an intense body of work that gives us insights into first-hand experiences of trench warfare. In much of this poetry we can trace a graph of changing attitudes towards the war. The exercises that follow introduce the poetry of the First World War, so that the reader of *Birdsong* can compare Faulks's treatment of the experience of war with that of some poets of the First World War. For the purposes of this reading it would be helpful to have access to the anthologies *Up the Line to Death*, edited by Brian Gardner (1976), and *The Penguin Book of First World War Poetry*, edited by Jon Silkin (1979).

READ . . .

— Read Rupert Brooke's sonnet sequence *1914*. In the sonnet 'Peace', why does the speaker welcome war? Brooke's sonnet sequence was widely read and admired during the war, but his critics say that these poems, written very early on in the war, are sentimental. One such critic was Charles Hamilton Sorley, who said that Brooke had 'clothed his attitude in fine words, but he has taken the sentimental attitude'. Compare Brooke's 'The Dead' with Sorley's 'When you see millions of the mouthless dead'. In particular, compare the tone, imagery and handling of the sonnet form. Both men died in 1915. Although patriotic verse was written and published in British newspapers throughout the war, there was a noticeable shift in attitudes towards the war in much of the poetry written from 1916 onwards. The ignorance of people at home and the incompetence of senior ranks were particular sources of bitterness (see Siegfried's Sassoon's 'Does it Matter?', 'Base Details' and 'The General' for well-known examples).

Most poets were public schoolboys, trained like Brooke or Sorley to write in traditional verse forms. They struggled to find new forms of expression that were adequate to convey the full intensity of their experiences in the trenches. Read Sassoon's 'Counter-Attack', which includes graphic images of corpses. Are these images made to serve the poem's effects, or are they too direct, too photographic, to be contained? The retainer that literature seems to have put on these public-school poets was challenged almost from the start by Isaac Rosenberg, a working-class Londoner. Read his poem 'Break of Day in the Trenches' and assess how he achieves more subtle effects than Sassoon, using tone and imagery. The poetry of the First World War was probably at least as influential as contemporary photographs in forming our ideas about the ordinary soldiers' experiences of war. Are there images in these war poems that find echoes in Faulks's novel?

VINTAGE
LIVING
TEXTS

Charlotte Gray

IN CLOSE-UP

Reading guides for

CHARLOTTE GRAY

BEFORE YOU BEGIN TO READ
— Look at the interview with Faulks and read the section on *Charlotte Gray*. You will see there that Faulks identifies a number of themes, including:

- How the past affects and influences the present
- Moral responsibility in personal decisions
- Risk
- War and its effects
- Memory
- Redemption.

Other themes that are relevant to the book might include:

- The concept of heroism and the nature of courage
- Love
- Men and women
- Innocence and optimism
- Desire and death.

Reading activities: detailed analysis

PART ONE. EARLY 1942.
CHAPTER 1 (pp. 1–7)

Focus on: openings

CONSIDER . . .
— Analyse the ways in which we are invited into this story. What is it about this opening that makes you want to go on reading?

Focus on: setting

ASK YOURSELF . . .
— How do you know where you are, in terms of setting and environment? What words and phrases supply you with that knowledge? And what resources of your own do you draw on? What elements in your own cultural background are there to help you orientate yourself in relation to this scene? Why is this setting one that is so familiar to us?

Focus on: language and vocabulary

PICK OUT . . .
— The first two words of this chapter are the name of a character who will become an important figure as the novel

unfolds. The third word is 'kicked', a verb with violent connotations. Underline or write down all the verbs and adverbs
in this chapter that convey an atmosphere of violence, aggres-
sion or destruction. Why might these verbs and adverbs be
necessary in this context? What effect does the build-up of
such words have on you as the reader?

Focus on: the body and sensation

DEFINE . . .

— There are a number of references to physical experiences
of various kinds in this chapter, most of them of an extreme
kind. Early on, we learn that the weather is cold, and throughout
there are allusions to bodily reactions and experiences. How
does this help the reader to relate to Peter Gregory's situation
on this flight? How much of a connection is made here between
what he might feel and what anyone might feel if they were
in a similar position? (Though, of course, most of us would
never experience something of this kind.)

Focus on: the gestures of heroism

EVALUATE THE EFFECTIVENESS OF UNDERSTATEMENT . . .
Look at the final words of the chapter on p. 7. '"How was it,
Greg?" "It was cold."' We know – because we have just read
this chapter – that Peter Gregory's experience in this night
flight was more than just one of being 'cold', or coping with
cold weather. Why does he answer in this way? What does his
understatement say about the way in which he is 'performing'
heroism?

COMPARE AND CONTRAST . . .

— Try to remember any films you have seen made either at
the time of the Second World War or since, where daring night-
flight raids of this kind are depicted. Compare those scenes

with this one. How far is Faulks's own scenario dependent on his readers already being familiar with just such a set-up, learned from films?

PART ONE
CHAPTER 2 (pp. 8–15)

Focus on: characterisation

DESCRIBE AND DISCERN . . .
— This is our first encounter with Charlotte Gray, who will turn out to be the eponymous heroine of the novel. Reread the description of her physical appearance and consider how this initial portrait influences your attitudes to her.

NOTE DOWN . . .
— Jot down the reference to Charlotte's father on p. 10, where she tells Cannerley and Morris that she moved to Edinburgh when her father took up a post in a hospital there. Look also for the second reference to Charlotte's father that appears in this chapter. You will need these pieces of information later.

ASSESS, COMPARE AND IMAGINE . . .
— Richard Cannerley and Robin Morris are portraits of a particular kind of privileged middle-class Englishman. Going on the information you are given about them in the course of this chapter (e.g. that they play golf, that they enjoy good wine, that Dick is married to someone called 'Celia', that they socialise with politicians and journalists, that they belong to gentlemen's clubs, etc.), work out your own imaginary curriculum vitae for each of them. What did their fathers do? Where did they go to school? And college? And so on. Then ask yourself why it is so easy to fill in this background detail? What stereotypes is

Faulks working with here? And where else might you find similarly stereotyped characters of this 'old school' type?

Focus on: language and reference

IMAGINE . . .
— Write out a dialogue between Dick and Robin as they play a game of golf. What phrases might they use about their game, or in chatting to each other, that most people would not use now? What words and phrases in the dialogue you have composed mark it explicitly as belonging to a certain historical period and a certain social class?

RESEARCH AND COMPARE . . .
— On p. 14 Dick Cannerley says, 'They also serve who only stand and wait.' This is a quotation from a famous poem by John Milton. Look up the source of the line in a *Dictionary of Quotations* and then read the poem; then read up on the occasion of Milton writing the poem. In what ways do the sentiments of the poem connect to the historical situation in 1942? How seriously is Cannerley making the connection?

RESEARCH . . .
— This chapter ends with the line 'England was blacked out and afraid'. Find out about 'the black-out' ordered throughout England during periods of the war. Ask someone who lived through it. Or read up about it. What does it mean? How was it done? Why? For what purpose? After you've found out about the practical side of this exercise, consider the metaphorical implications of a phrase like 'blacked out'. Consider, too, the practical and psychological implications of living under such conditions.

PART ONE
CHAPTER 3, FIRST SECTION (pp. 16–21)

*Focus on: atmosphere, setting and the
construction of gender*

COMPARE AND CONTRAST . . .

— Here we are offered a 'girls' scene', as opposed to the 'boys' scene' that opened the novel. Look back at Chapter 1 on pp. 1–7 and compare the presentation of the two settings. What might be distinctively 'masculine' about the opening section, and distinctively 'feminine' about the later passages introducing Daisy, Charlotte and Sally? Pick out the words and phrases that give you these clues.

IMAGINE AND DESCRIBE . . .

— Using the paragraph on p. 20 that tells you about Sally's room, write a description of what you think she might be like: physically, emotionally, professionally. Then do the same with the paragraph that describes Daisy's room on the same page.

PART ONE
CHAPTER 3, SECOND SECTION (pp. 21–2)

Focus on: the theme of how the past influences the present

NOTE AND RECALL . . .

— There are number of clues sewn into this little section. If you have already read Faulks's *Birdsong*, then some of this information may make sense to you. Take five minutes to think about how the two novels relate to each other, and where you have met Charlotte's father before.

DETECT AND DISCERN . . .

— There are two odd references in this section. The first is on p. 21, where Amelia Gray is said to feel that Charlotte's nature is such that she possesses an 'almost excessive reticence, a lack of trust, from whose likely cause her mother turned her gaze away'. The second allusion is on p. 22, where we are told that Amelia knows that 'she had failed her daughter'. Remember these hints; you will need them later.

Focus on: allusion

RESEARCH . . .

— On p. 21 we are told that Amelia thought of 'Nessus and his shirt of flame' when she reflected on her husband and his particular emotional and psychological state when he was on leave from the Front in 1916. Look up Nessus in a dictionary of classical reference. Who was he? What does this connection suggest about Gray's state of mind at this time?

PART ONE
CHAPTER 3, THIRD SECTION (pp. 23–30)

Focus on: the theme of chance

ASK YOURSELF . . .

— This is the first time that Charlotte Gray and Peter Gregory meet, though we have met each of them before. What do you make of this first introduction? Is it promising, as things now stand?

— Once you have read to the end of the novel, look back again at this section and see if you have changed your mind about any elements of this originating scene and its sense of what may be possible.

PART ONE
CHAPTER 4 (pp. 31–8)

Focus on: the theme of parallel lives

COMPARE . . .

You will see that the two sections of this chapter begin with the same sentence structure: the name of a character, the verb and the scene. On p. 31 we read, 'Peter Gregory was sitting in a wooden barrack-room in southern England'. On p. 35 we read, 'Charlotte Gray was drinking tea in the kitchen'.

— In what other ways do the two sections of this chapter connect to each other? You might look for things like the fact that in both cases we hear about childhood memories; or that we hear about how Peter and Charlotte feel about other people, and how they relate to their friends. We also learn how they both react to the deaths that are happening around them; and we find out, in both cases, about a certain idealism that they both possess that seems 'worth fighting for' (p. 31). Make a list of as many of these examples as you can find.

*Focus on: the theme of memory
and the development of character*

RESEARCH . . .

— On p. 37 we are told that Charlotte was given a copy of Marcel Proust's famous series of novels entitled *A la recherche du temps perdu* (1913–27), generally known by C.K. Scott-Moncrieff's English translation, *Remembrance of Things Past* (1922–31). The first book in the series is called *Du Côté de chez Swann* (1913), or *Swann's Way*. Find out as much as you can about this book. Read the beginning, or even read the whole novel. How does this reference help you to understand: a. Charlotte's romantic attitude to all things French? and b. the treatment of the ideal of France in the novel as a whole?

— And when you have read the opening of *Swann's Way*, consider why it might be that Charlotte is described on p. 38 as needing 'no forcing of remembrance' and how she was able to remember the taste of 'the red wine from the rue de Tournon'.

PART ONE
CHAPTER 5 (pp. 39–49)

Focus on: characterisation

ASSESS AND REMEMBER . . .

— In this section we learn two key things about Charlotte: the character of her passion for Peter Gregory, which she experiences as 'anguish' (p. 42), and that she views life 'as a narrative' (p. 44). When you have finished reading the whole novel, look back at these two sections and consider how these clues have coloured all of Charlotte's decisions and actions in the course of the story.

RESEARCH AND NOTE FOR FUTURE REFERENCE . . .

— When Charlotte looks at Dr Wolf and his patient on p. 43 she thinks that they resemble 'two figures from de Chirico lost in a giant piazza'. Look at the interview with Sebastian Faulks included earlier in this book and read the section where he speaks about de Chirico's paintings. Research this painter and his work: the Tate Gallery in London – both Tate Britain and the Tate Modern – holds examples. How you do react to the special quality of his strange paintings?

Focus on: the theme of moral responsibility

CONSIDER AND INTERPRET . . .

— Read the section on p. 46 where Dr Wolf and Charlotte discuss the moral culpability of the French, who have capitulated to the demands of the occupying German forces, and have even collaborated with them. Analyse Dr Wolf's argument that such collaborators are 'worse' than the Nazis. How do you react to this? Ask yourself how far it is necessary to stand up for one's independence in a time of war? What do notions of 'honour' mean to you? Consider how this question is dealt with in different ways throughout the novel as a whole.

Focus on: narrative structure

REWRITE . . .

— On pp. 40–2 and 47–8 we are told about one 'episode' in the novel – the occasion of the party in Ralph's attic room – though these two accounts of that one event are separated by the story of what is happening to Charlotte and to Peter ten days later. What impact does this divided account of the episode make?

— Now rewrite the whole story of that episode at the party from the point of view of Daisy, and from the point of view of Ralph. What does each of them notice about what is going on between Charlotte and Peter? How does this exercise help you to assess the twin focus of Peter's and Charlotte's perceptions of what happens at the party?

PART ONE
CHAPTER 6 (pp. 50–66)

Focus on: language

ANALYSE SEMANTICS AND CONNOTATION . . .

Language is a 'structured system for communicating meanings'. Semantics is the study of how those meanings are created, not just in terms of grammar and dictionary definitions, but also in the sense of understood (or implied) meanings, often dependent on the context. A technical term like 'connotation' will help you to identify implied meanings, such as the positive or negative impact of particular words in particular contexts.

— Look at these sentences: 'Go ahead. Leave me to do the washing up.' Strictly speaking, this comprises two instructions: one giving permission, or agreeing, and the other giving information about the division of labour. But what do you understand that it means? Read it out loud in different tones of voice, so that you can give it a positive and a negative connotation.

— Now look at the brief exchange between Peter and Borowski on p. 52. What is the difference in connotation between a *French* mistress, and a French *mistress*?

ANALYSE MORPHOLOGY . . .

Morphology is the technical term for changes in word formation. New words – neologisms – enter the language all the time, as borrowings from other languages, as acronyms (made up of initial letters), as compound words (where two existing words are put together), as well as in many other ways. Words also change their meaning. In the 1920s what would 'gay' have meant? Or 'wicked'? What do these words mean now?

— Look at the passage on p. 57 where Cannerley is talking to Charlotte:

'Lots of smart young women are doing their bit, you know,' he said. 'The FANYS are as posh as Queen Charlotte's ball. You needn't think it *infra dig*.'
'That isn't what I thought at all. I'm not a snob . . .'

— Now consider these words and phrases from that exchange: smart, doing their bit, FANYS, posh, Queen Charlotte's ball, *infra dig*, snob. Look up each of these words and phrases in a dictionary and consider where it comes from, or how it has been created through morphology. Here are some technical labels to help you:

- Acronym: making a word out of initial letters (there are two in this passage)
- Borrowing: from another language
- clipping: making a word, or a comprehensible phrase, by cutting it down (as in 'mike' for 'microphone').

— Look for other examples as you read the novel as a whole. How far is Faulks using the distinctive slang of the time to create a period flavour?

Focus on: narrative method

ANALYSE . . .
— Chapter 6 is made up of eight short passages (pp. 50–2; 52–5; 55–7; 57–9; 59–60; 60–2; 62–5; and 65–6). Look at the openings and endings of each of those passages. How does the narrative structure convey a sense of sexual tension? What specific references and allusions build towards the sex scene at the end of the chapter?

PART ONE
CHAPTER 7 (pp. 67–76)

Focus on: allusion and reference

RESEARCH . . .

On p. 67 Peter Gregory is given the task of reading a children's book called *Le Petit Prince* (1943) by Antoine de Saint-Exupéry. On p. 68 we are told that the furnishings of Madame Fanon's borrowed flat include bookshelves 'packed with the novels of Warwick Deeping and Hugh Walpole'.

— Find out about these authors. *The Little Prince* is a famous book with a cult following. You may already have read it. But Saint-Exupéry also wrote a number of novels for adults, with titles like (in English) *Night Flight* (1932), *Wind, Sand and Stars* (1939) and *Flight to Arras* (1942). Why, therefore, has Faulks picked this particular book for Gregory to read?

Warwick Deeping's best-known work was *Sorrell and Son* (1925). Hugh Walpole was another popular novelist during the inter-war years, but in both cases their work is not so fashionable now.

— In what ways might the values and ideals expressed in the work of Saint-Exupéry or Deeping or Walpole help to focus the values and ideals of the war years that Faulks is exploring in his novel as a whole?

PART ONE
CHAPTER 8 (pp. 77–85)

Focus on: narrative structure and literary clues

COMPARE . . .

— Read the beginning of this chapter where the narrator

describes Charlotte's 'depression' and refers obliquely to its source. Then read the end of the chapter where there is also a reference to Charlotte's personal need to 'understand herself . . . away from the doleful influence of her parents', so that she can 'see how things had gone wrong in her life'. Then look back at p. 21 where reference is made to Charlotte's 'excessive reticence' and 'lack of trust', and to p. 22 where the narrator tells us that her mother felt that she had 'failed her daughter'. — What does the build-up of these clues suggest to you? Remember that Charlotte knows whatever it is that she knows — and we are meant to feel that she is not altogether certain of what it is that causes her depression or these traits in her character. Remember, too, that the omniscient narrator does know — or seem to know — where this is leading.

RESEARCH . . .
— As Charlotte is finding her way back from her meeting with 'Mr Jackson' she is said to use the 'falling numbers on the bedroom doors' as 'her simple thread back from the minotaur'. Look up this allusion. Why is it relevant at this particular moment, both to Charlotte's specific situation and to our position as readers of a text where certain things are being revealed while others are concealed?

PART ONE
CHAPTER 9 (pp. 86–98)

Focus on: clues and narrative structure

ADD TO YOUR LIST . . .
— While Charlotte is being examined by Dr Burch she has a moment of memory — analepsis is the technical term for this — when she recalls seeing another doctor when she was a

teenager. This occurs on pp. 95–6. Keep this moment in mind, along with the other 'clues' to a narrative shape and to the unfolding of Charlotte's character.

Focus on: characterisation

ASK YOURSELF . . .

— Look at the section on pp. 86–7 on the ways in which Charlotte attempts to make a 'routine' out of her infrequent meetings with Peter Gregory. What does this need suggest about her character? How does it relate to the section in Chapter 5 (p. 44) where we are told that Charlotte views life as 'a narrative'?

TRY OUT . . .

— Write out the list of words that the psychologist uses to test Charlotte on p. 97. Try out the same process of free association on yourself, then on one of your friends. How revealing do you think such a test might be? What, in your opinion, is the most significant and revealing answer in Charlotte's list here? Think especially about her reaction to the key word 'father'.

— You might also like to have a go at this test. Make sure you answer the questions as you go along. The interpretations are in the Contexts section for *Charlotte Gray*. Don't cheat and look at them before answering. Go through them slowly and do one exercise at a time. Don't look ahead. Get a pencil and some paper to write down your answers as you go along. You will need this record at the end.

1. Put the following five animals in the order of your preference.

a. Cow b. Tiger c. Sheep d. Horse e. Pig

2. Write one word that describes each one of the following:
    a. Dog. b. Cat c. Rat d. Coffee e. Sea

3. Think of someone (who knows you and is important to you) whom you can relate to the following colours. Do not use the same answer twice. Name just one person for each colour.
    a. Yellow b. Orange c. Red d. White e. Green

Finished? Please be sure that your answers are what you *really want* them to be. Now look up the interpretations in the Contexts section. How effectively do you think this test reveals your personality? How does it compare with the one used by Dr Burch?

READ AND COMPARE . . .
— Read this translation of an extract from an article by Sigmund Freud about the 'Forgetting of Foreign Words'. It is taken from an essay entitled 'On the Psychopathology of Everyday Life', which was first published in 1901. Freud here uses a technique of 'free association' in order to work out the secret that is troubling the young man to whom he is speaking. Compare his analysis with your own analysis of yourself according to Dr Burch's system, or with your reading of Charlotte's character.

> Last summer – it was once again on a holiday trip –
> I renewed my acquaintance with a certain young
> man of academic background. I soon found that he
> was familiar with some of my psychological publica-
> tions. We had fallen into conversation – how I have
> now forgotten – about the social status of the race
> to which we both belonged; and ambitious feelings
> prompted him to give vent to a regret that his

generation was doomed (as he expressed it) to atrophy, and could not develop its talents or satisfy its needs. He ended a speech of impassioned fervour with the well-known line of Virgil's in which the unhappy Dido commits to posterity her vengeance on Aeneas: '*Exoriare . . .*' Or rather, he *wanted* to end it in this way, for he could not get hold of the quotation and tried to conceal an obvious gap in what he remembered by changing the order of the words: '*Exoriar(e) ex nostris ossibus ultor.*' At last he said irritably: 'Please don't look so scornful: you seem as if you were gloating over my embarrassment. Why not help me? There's something missing in the line; how does the whole thing really go?'

'I'll help you with pleasure,' I replied, and gave the quotation in its correct form: '*Exoriar(e)* ALIQUIS *nostris ex ossibus ultor.*'

'How stupid to forget a word like that! By the way, you claim that one never forgets a thing without some reason. I should be very curious to learn how I came to forget the indefinite pronoun "*aliquis*" in this case.'

I took up this challenge most readily, for I was hoping for a contribution to my collection. So I said: 'That should not take us long. I must only ask you to tell me, *candidly* and *uncritically*, whatever comes into your mind if you direct your attention to the forgotten word without any definite aim.'

'Good. There springs to my mind, then, the ridiculous notion of dividing up the word like this: *a* and *liquis.*'

'What does that mean?' 'I don't know.' 'And what occurs to you next?' 'What comes next is *Reliquien* [relics], *liquefying, fluidity, fluid*. Have you discovered anything so far?'

'No. Not by any means yet. But go on.'

'I am thinking', he went on with a scornful laugh, 'of *Simon of Trent*, whose relics I saw two years ago in a church at Trent. I am thinking of the accusation of ritual blood-sacrifice which is being brought against the Jews again just now, and of *Kleinpaul*'s book [1892] in which he regards all these supposed victims as incarnations, one might say new editions, of the Saviour.'

'The notion is not entirely unrelated to the subject we were discussing before the Latin word slipped your memory.'

'True. My next thoughts are about an article that I read lately in an Italian newspaper. Its title, I think, was "What St *Augustine* says about Women". What do you make of that?'

'I am waiting.'

'And now comes something that is quite clearly unconnected with our subject.'

'Please refrain from any criticism and –'

'Yes, I understand. I am thinking of a fine old gentleman I met on my travels last week. He was a real *original*, with all the appearance of a huge bird of prey. His name was *Benedict*, if it's of interest to you.'

'Anyhow, here are a row of saints and Fathers of the Church: St *Simon*, St *Augustine*, St *Benedict*. There was, I think, a Church Father called *Origen*. Moreover, three of these names are also first names, like *Paul* in *Kleinpaul*.'

'Now it's St *Januarius* and the miracle of his blood that comes into my mind – my thoughts seem to me to be running on mechanically.'

'Just a moment: St *Januarius* and St *Augustine* both have to do with the calendar. But won't you remind me about the miracle of his blood?'

'Surely you must have heard of that? They keep the blood of St Januarius in a phial inside a church at Naples, and on a particular holy day it miraculously *liquefies*. The people attach great importance to this miracle and get very excited if it's delayed, as happened once at a time when the French were occupying the town. So the general in command – or have I got it wrong? was it Garibaldi? – took the reverend gentleman aside and gave him to understand, with an unmistakable gesture towards the soldiers posted outside, that he *hoped* the miracle would take place very soon. And in fact it did take place . . .'

'Well, go on. Why do you pause?'

'Well, something *has* come into my mind . . . but it's too intimate to pass on . . . Besides, I don't see any connection, or any necessity for saying it.'

'You can leave the connection to me. Of course I can't force you to talk about something that you find distasteful; but then you mustn't insist on learning from me how you came to forget your *aliquis*.'

'Really? Is that what you think? Well then, I've suddenly thought of a lady from whom I might easily hear a piece of news that would be very awkward for both of us.'

'That her periods have stopped?'

'How could you guess that?'

'That's not difficult any longer; you've prepared the way sufficiently. Think of *the calendar saints, the blood that starts to flow on a particular day, the disturbance when the event fails to take place, the open threats that the miracle must be vouchsafed, or else* . . . In fact you've made use of the miracle of St Januarius to manufacture a brilliant allusion to women's periods.'

'Without being aware of it. And you really mean to say that it was this anxious expectation that made me unable to produce an unimportant word like *aliquis*?'

'It seems to me undeniable. You need only recall the division you made into *a-liquis*, and your associations: *relics, liquefying, fluid*. St Simon was *sacrificed as a child* – shall I go on and show how he comes in? You were led on to him by the subject of relics.'

'No, I'd much rather you didn't. I hope you don't take these thoughts of mine too seriously, if indeed I really had them. In return I will confess to you that the lady is Italian and that I went to Naples with her. But mayn't all this just be a matter of chance?'

'I must leave it to your own judgement to decide whether you can explain all these connections by the assumption that they are matters of chance. I can however tell you that every case like this that you care to analyse will lead you to "matters of chance" that are just as striking.'

PART ONE
CHAPTER 10 (pp. 99–116)

Focus on: the theme of emotion in war

COMPARE AND CONTRAST . . .
— Peter and Charlotte both experience dramatic representations of emotion in this chapter: he on p. 103, she on pp. 113–16. Compare their two reactions to similar situations,

where each imagines that they will not see the other again. What is the effect of the parallel presentation of their separate experiences within a short space of time? Where else have you seen this technique used in the novel as whole?

RESEARCH AND COMPARE . . .
— Read *Testament of Youth* (1933) by Vera Brittain. This is a true account of her experiences during the First World War. Look particularly at the passage where she describes how she hears of the death at the Front of her fiancé Roland Leighton. This is also the result of a telephone conversation, in this case with Roland's mother. How does Brittain's true story compare with this fictional version?

LOOK BACK AND FORWARD . . .
— Another clue to difficult events in Charlotte's past is given to us on pp. 111–12. What is the significance of us being told a little bit more about her vague memories just at this moment in her story?

PART ONE
CHAPTER 11 (pp. 117–23)

Focus on: image and metaphor

CONSIDER . . .
— On p. 100 Peter tells Charlotte of the pilot's code word for the moon. He refers to it in his little farewell note on p. 102. Now Charlotte herself thinks of it as she looks at the moon on p. 123. Bear this link in mind. What metaphoric and imaginative connections are implied? If 'Charlotte' is code for 'the moon', what is suggested by her surname of 'Gray'? In what ways – given that we now know that Charlotte is about

to go to France as an undercover agent – is this an appropriate name for her?

PART ONE

Looking over Part One

QUESTIONS FOR DISCUSSION OR ESSAYS

1. *Charlotte Gray* is a novel that relies for its impact on the evocation of a particular period feel. In what specific ways does Faulks create that setting and mood?

2. The narrative structure of *Charlotte Gray* is often made up of parallel stories where two characters are apart, but thinking of the same, or similar, things – perhaps even of each other. Look out two such passages and compare and contrast them.

3. How does this novel set out questions of gender difference? Is that difference accentuated by the war situation? If so, how?

4. Discuss some of the metaphorical or literary devices that Faulks uses to create tension in his narrative.

5. *Charlotte Gray* is related to us by an ominiscient narrator, though the perspective is most often Charlotte's own. What are the strengths of this method? And what might be the weaknesses?

PART TWO. SUMMER 1942.
CHAPTER I (pp. 127–48)

Focus on: point of view

COLLECT EXAMPLES AND ASSESS . . .

— In this chapter we encounter a new place, time and perspective. Although this part is told in the third person, the point of view (for the first section) is that of André Duguay. Write down all the words and phrases that make you aware that this is a very young child. Some of them will actually be to do with his body, like the 'baby whiteness' of his skin on p. 127. Others will be to do with his attitudes and understanding, as 'in the rough diagram of his understanding animals were with children against an adult world of rules and obligations', on the same page. How effective is this method of conveying the mind of a child?

ANALYSE . . .

— Consider how many times the point of view shifts in this chapter. Sometimes it's André's; sometimes it is the perspective of the narrator – when we are told about the history of Lavaurette, for instance; and sometimes it is Julien Levade's. What effect does this changing range of perspectives have? How much information are we given, and how effectively is the atmosphere conveyed?

Focus on: the theme of moral courage

CONSIDER THE USE OF IRONY . . .

— Look at the scene in Madame Galliot's shop on pp. 131–3. How much information are we given here about what is happening? How are our reactions manipulated by the fact that there are adults here dealing with a child? The scene is ironic, but it could also be described in other ways. Consider which of these words most appropriately describes the moral tone of this section: pathetic, angry, sceptical, critical, cynical, indifferent, approving?

DISCUSS . . .

— 'It's nothing to do with the hôtel de ville,' says the clerk at the Town Hall (p. 135). 'It's nothing to do with us,' says Bernard the policeman (p. 137). Look through this chapter – and count up how many times such self-excusing phrases are used. How does this repetition make you react? Once you have got the picture of an Occupied country collaborating with an overbearing enemy, you might like to consider (or debate if you are in a group) how you would like to behave in similar circumstances – and how you feel you would behave.

— Look back at Charlotte's discussion about Occupied France with Dr Wolf on p. 46. How does that episode relate to this one? Look for other places in the novel where these moral issues are debated.

Focus on: the theme of racial difference and 'ethnic cleansing'

RESEARCH . . .

— On pp. 133 and 135 we learn that 'they' have painted a yellow Star of David in the door of the Duguays' house. What does this mean? What is the point of it? Research other examples from history where ethnic groups are required to identify themselves in some way. How do you feel about this? Does it still go on? Look up the phrase 'ethnic cleansing' in a dictionary. To what does it refer, who coined it and to what historical situation does it relate? In the Contexts section for *Charlotte Gray* you will find an extract from a leader in *The Times*, dated 23 May 2001. Read that extract and consider how the situation described there relates to the one portrayed in Faulks's novel.

Focus on: period, setting, atmosphere

DISCRIMINATE . . .

— Look carefully through this chapter and note down each time that any kind of food is mentioned. How do these descriptions help to convey the period atmosphere of provincial Occupied France in 1942?

PART TWO
CHAPTER 2 (pp. 149–71)

Focus on: the theme of converging lives and narrative structure

COMPARE AND CONTRAST . . .

— This chapter is made up of nine short sections, mainly giving alternating narratives that switch between Charlotte's perspective and Julien's – with one exception where the omniscient narrator tells us about Sylvie Cariteau, her mother and the Duguay boys. So it goes: Charlotte, pp. 149–51; Charlotte, pp. 151–6; Julien, pp. 156–8; Charlotte, pp. 158–9; Julien, pp. 159–61; Charlotte pp. 161–6; Charlotte and Julien, pp. 166–8; André and the Cariteaus, pp. 168–70; and Charlotte, pp. 170–1.

— How does the build-up of these sections help to depict the convergence of Charlotte's and Julien's life? What parallels can you find between the sections? For instance, Charlotte's sections on pp. 149–56 deal with Jackson's elaborate preparation of her 'story' as 'Dominique Guilbert' and her physical transformation. Then Julien's section on pp. 156–8 tells about the possible physical realisation of another 'story' in Julien's work on converting the monastery into a hotel. So the themes of the two sections work together. Look for other examples like this. Then ask yourself why the section on pp. 168–170 that focuses on the Cariteaus is also included.

Focus on: allusion

COMPARE . . .

— Look back at the reference on p. 37 where we are told about Charlotte's reading of Proust. On pp. 163–4 we are told more about Charlotte's attitude to the book. Keep a note of each time the book is mentioned and build up a picture, not only of *Remembrance of Things Past*, but of Charlotte's perception of what it means to her and how it influences her view of France.

Focus on: the theme of emotional release in times of danger

RESEARCH . . .

— As Charlotte's parachute lands, she feels 'the irresistible uprising of happiness' (p. 166). Read David Hare's play *Plenty* (1978). It is about a woman who also worked in the secret service during the war, and about what happens to her after the war. Compare the fictional portrayal of Susan's emotional life, while under the pressure of her deceptions and in danger, with Charlotte's.

PART TWO
CHAPTER 3 (pp. 172–85)

Focus on: sense of place

ANALYSE . . .

— If you look at the interview with Faulks, you will see that he speaks about houses, and how envisaging those houses helps to give substance to the atmosphere and character that he is trying to create. Look carefully at this description of the house where Levade lives. Analyse how the architectural characteristics of the house help to fill out the picture of Levade's character.

Focus on: the theme of moral responsibility

CONTRAST . . .

— Look at the passage on p. 175 where Charlotte reads the newspaper and begins to form an impression of life under Occupation. Why does her reading make her 'queasy'? What do you think of the way the national press are handling the situation? Now look at the long passage that ends the chapter on pp. 180–5, where Oliver Cresswell and Richard Cannerley discuss their plan to use Charlotte to drop false information to one group of resistance fighters. On p. 185 Cannerley thinks, 'I am a coward . . . I'm trapped and I'm too frightened to move.' In what ways is Cannerley's position similar to that of the collaborating press in Occupied France? In what ways is it different?

PART TWO
CHAPTER 4 (pp. 186–201)

Focus on: characterisation

ANALYSE . . .

— Most of this chapter is given over to telling the story of Charlotte's visit to Limoges and to Ussel, but there is also a lot of information about Charlotte herself, her reactions, her feelings, her likes and dislikes. Go carefully through the chapter listing the elements that you learn about her here: for instance, her methodicalness in laying out her possessions (pp. 186–7), her disgust at the bidet concealed behind a 'greasy curtain' (p. 187), her washing herself 'scrupulously' in the bathroom (p. 187). Then analyse this list of traits and consider how Faulks has used this chapter to add to the picture of Charlotte's character.

COMPARE . . .

— If you look at pp. 189–91 you will see that the only section in this chapter to deal with Julien's point of view is devoted to explaining his new sense of moral responsibility and his determination to help the Duguay children. Now look at pp. 199–200, where Antoinette explains to Charlotte how and why she became a wireless operator for the French resistance. How do these two explanations of moral choice relate to each other? And how do they relate to Charlotte's own position? What qualities might these three characters have in common?

PART TWO
CHAPTER 5 (pp. 202–10)

Focus on: the theme of responsibility and trust

DISCUSS . . .

— How might the three short sections in this chapter relate to each other? The first consists of the meeting and conversation between Levade and AnneMarie; the second is Julien's conversation with 'the Communist'; the third is Charlotte's journey to, and meeting with, Monsieur Chollet.

PART TWO
CHAPTER 6 (pp. 211–22)

Focus on: the theme of love and risk

ADD UP AND MAKE A PATTERN . . .

— Write down all the examples in this chapter where characters are described as doing something risky out of love, and doing it often with some small consideration for the endangered others whom they protect. Examples might include Sylvie Cariteau buying the sheet music for André (p. 211); Julien letting Charlotte sleep in his bed (p. 215); the behaviour of the farming couple who have sheltered Peter Gregory (pp. 216–17). Then link these examples to the two passages on pp. 219 and 221 where Charlotte first thinks about what she is doing by staying in France, and why, and when she explains herself (a bit) to Julien. Try to make as many connections as you can between these different instances of generosity. What cumulative effect does this narrative technique bring about as it tells you similar things without making explicit comparisons?

Focus on: allusion and the theme of memory

RESEARCH . . .

— On p. 218 we are told that Charlotte 'took an end bread from the remains of lunch on the table, dipped it in the tea and sucked. No gateway of unconscious memory swung gloriously open . . .' If you look at the opening passage of Marcel Proust's *Remembrance of Things Past* you will see that Faulks's allusion is to this scene. Add this to your list of references in his series of novels. And then consider how the theme of memory is played out in the novel *Charlotte Gray* as a whole.

123

PART TWO
CHAPTER 7 (pp. 223–34)

Focus on: the theme of storytelling

RESEARCH AND COMPARE . . .

— At the end of this chapter Charlotte goes to bed with 'a dry taste in her mouth . . . the taste, she thought bitterly, of fantasy' (p. 234). Now look back at the moment when Charlotte is trying to convince Monsieur Chollet that she is not a collaborator or a secret policewoman, and so resorts to speaking English to show that she is prepared to take risks. In English, she begins to tell him the story of Cinderella (p. 209), but finds she has difficulty remembering it. Now – arriving to stay at the Domaine – Charlotte feels 'as though she had seen it many times before . . . if she could spend long enough in this house, she seemed to feel, it might reveal to her some lost plan or harmony' (p. 223).

— Taking these two references as your cue, look at p. 229, where Charlotte is retelling stories from classical legend to entertain André and Jacob. Look up some of these stories; that of Icarus; Persephone; Hector and Ajax and Achilles and their exploits in the Trojan War; Odysseus and his long journey home to Ithaca. When you have done that, try to imagine how the events of those other stories might be compared to the events of Charlotte's own story.

PART TWO
CHAPTER 8 (pp. 235–41)

Focus on: narrative structure

CONSIDER . . .

— Benech has been already been briefly introduced. What is the effect of the narrative method which now fleshes out the portrayal of his character and his attitudes and beliefs? What signals does this give out to the reader, hinting at what might be to come?

— Now look at the section on pp. 240–1 where Peter Gregory is shown leaving the old couple who have been sheltering him. And then look back at the final section of the chapter that ended Part One, on pp. 120–3. At the end of Part One the narrative focused on Charlotte. At the end of Part Two the narrative focuses on Peter. How do the two sections compare? In what ways are they similar? And what ways different? What narrative patterns are being built up?

PART TWO

Looking over Part Two

QUESTIONS FOR DISCUSSION OR ESSAYS

1. 'My subject is war, and the pity of war.' How is this theme played out in *Charlotte Gray*?

2. Consider the themes of moral responsibility and personal commitment. In what ways are these issues discussed in the novel, and in what ways is the judgement of the reader manipulated by the narrative method?

3. '*Charlotte Gray* is a solidly nineteenth-century sort of title.' Why might the Faulks novel be compared to the nineteenth-century model? Do you agree?

4. Analyse either the treatment of food or clothes in this section of the novel. How do Faulks's descriptions work to convey the period setting?

5. Some critics have described Sebastian Faulks as a 'feminine' novelist. What do you think they mean? Do you agree?

PART THREE. AUTUMN–WINTER 1942–3.
CHAPTER I (pp. 245–57)

Focus on: vocabulary and setting

DISTINGUISH AND ILLUSTRATE . . .
— Throughout this chapter the way that words are used and misused is made a subject of irony and of scene-setting. Distinguish the ways in which Robin Morris and Richard Cannerley use words from the ways that words are used by Charlotte and Julien. Obviously their two situations are different, but can you illustrate that difference with specific examples?

Focus on: characterisation and narrative patterns

COMPARE . . .
— On p. 245 Julien says, 'You're a remarkable woman, aren't you, Madame Guilbert?' Look back over the novel. Where has this been said to Charlotte previously, by whom and why? What does the fact that the narrative repeats this phrase suggest to you?

REWRITE AND SUMMARISE . . .

— Look at the last section of this chapter (pp. 256–7), which focuses on the perspective of Claude Benech. Now summarise the scene in the bar, but write your account in the voice of Roudil. There are a number of ironies in Benech's mistaken point of view. Once you have written out the scene from Roudil's perspective, compare it with Faulks's section and work out how he conveys Benech's skewed attitudes.

PART THREE
CHAPTER 2 (pp. 258–70)

Focus on: the theme of memory, storytelling and deception

EXAMINE . . .

— 'There were days when she scarcely thought of Peter Gregory, days when she convinced herself that he did not exist and that her memory of him was false; yet she still believed that only she could give him back his life and that only he could plausibly join her future to her past' (p. 259). In the course of this chapter Charlotte thinks about her past, and discusses the role of memory with Levade. Examine how the discussion of this theme is worked out.

DESCRIBE . . .

— How does the last section of this chapter (pp. 268–70) relate to the preceding passages? Describe the connections in terms of themes and plot structure.

Focus on: the themes of identity, self-construction and voyeurism

COMPARE . . .

— As Charlotte looks at herself in the mirror and redyes her hair to disguise herself as someone else, she thinks about who she is and the character of her self-constructed identity. Then, at the end of this scene, she feels that someone is watching her. If you have read Faulks's novel *The Girl at the Lion d'Or* you will know that scenes in bathrooms and the role of the voyeur appear there, too. Compare the presentation of these themes in the two novels.

PART THREE
CHAPTER 3 (pp. 271–88)

Focus on: the theme of fantasy and escape

INTERPRET . . .

— Each of the first five sections of this chapter depicts different kinds of fantasy or other means of imaginative 'escape' deployed by various different characters: Julien fantasises about his hotel and 'Dominique'; the children play with their toy soldiers; Claude Benech is enticed by dreams of his own significance; Levade analyses the terms of his existence; Charlotte dreams about food, and Julien about his relationship with her. Work out the connections across these sections. Now ask yourself why the final section brings us back to the realities of Peter Gregory's situation. What part does 'fantasy' play here, as opposed to in the earlier sections?

PART THREE
CHAPTER 4 (pp. 289–305)

Focus on: allusion and reference

OUTLINE, RESEARCH AND COMMENT ON . . .

— On pp. 289–90 there is a description of the painting of Levade's that he had given to Charlotte. If you look at the interview with Faulks, you will see that he says he was thinking of a de Chirico-style of painting. Remember that we have already had a reference to de Chirico's work earlier in the novel. What significance do this subject and style of painting – as described here – have in the novel as a whole?

— Charlotte's reading of Proust is also mentioned again in this chapter. How does this reference relate to the others? And how does this allusion contribute to the themes of memory and loss?

Focus on: the theme of parents and children

TRACE . . .

— Note down all the instances where relations between parents and children are described and discussed in this chapter. How does each one compare with the others? Note: these references are not always describing relations between actual families. Make sure you look out for words like 'maternal' as well.

PART THREE
CHAPTER 5 (pp. 306–27)

Focus on: setting and atmosphere

EVALUATE . . .

— There are a great number of descriptions of clothes, the

body and food in this chapter. How do they help to build the excitement and tension associated with 'the drop', and to max-imise the effect of the sex scene at the end?

PART THREE
CHAPTER 6 (pp. 328–47)

Focus on: the themes of memory and how the past affects the present

RESEARCH AND COMPARE . . .
Much of this chapter deals with the clues that have been accu-mulating around Charlotte's just-out-of-reach memory of what-ever it is that happened to her in her childhood. Here several layers that relate to this problem are set out in the narrative: Charlotte has a dream about her father; she confides what little she can recall to Levade; there is a scene from her childhood (pp. 336–9) that starts to be told from her point of view and then switches to give Gray's.
— If you have read Faulks's *Birdsong* you will know that 'Wraysford', briefly mentioned here (p. 337), is the hero of that novel. If you have not read *Birdsong*, then you might like to do so. Consider how the events of that novel are here influencing events in *Charlotte Gray*, just as the events of the First World War actually did influence events in the Second.

Focus on: the theme of moral responsibility

JUSTIFY AND DISCUSS . . .
— Julien says to Charlotte, 'Men like Benech are worse than the Germans' (p. 347). Why does he say this? What is it that makes Benech 'worse' than the occupying enemy? Discuss – in the light of the moral complexities that you have been shown

in the novel as a whole — whether or not you agree with this statement.

PART THREE
CHAPTER 7 (pp. 348–73)

Focus on: vocabulary and the language of officialdom

LIST AND EVALUATE . . .

— In the opening section of this chapter, where Pichon arrives to arrest Levade, there are a number of official phrases that he uses. Write these down and evaluate their 'real' meaning — if they were used in their simplest sense — and then consider how they are used to convey threats and to create a hierarchy of authority and law, which places Levade (and all Jews) on a lower scale.

Focus on: language

DEFINE, NOTE AND QUESTION . . .

— Read the last two pages (or any two pages) of this chapter. Underline every adjective that you find, and every adverb. You will see that there are very few of either, but — for the most part — more adverbs than adjectives. Why is this style of writing appropriate to this particular episode and to the events that are taking place here?

Focus on: the imagery of painting

RELATE . . .

— As Charlotte packs a case for Levade, she puts in the canvas of his own painting — the one he had shown her as an example of his best work (p. 362). Why does she do this? Look back at the description of the picture. Look forward to the episode that occurs later when Levade finds the canvas. What is the symbolic relation of this (imagined) painting to the novel as a whole?

PART THREE
CHAPTER 8 (pp. 374-79)

Focus on: the theme of communication and understanding

CONTRAST . . .

— Levade writes three letters: one to AnneMarie, one to Julien, and one to 'Dominique Guilbert' – that is, Charlotte. Compare and contrast the three letters. What is he trying to communicate to each of these three persons, and how does he go about doing so? Why does he put Julien's letter aside and then take it up again?

Focus on: irony and the theme of how the past affects the present

ACCOUNT FOR . . .

— Why does the narrative represent Levade's ironic turn of thought as he wonders if this wagon had once carried 'the very horse he had tried to eat'? Look back at his account of that episode (p. 340), and consider the implications of its being evoked at this moment in Levade's personal story.

PART THREE

Looking over Part Three

QUESTIONS FOR DISCUSSION OR ESSAYS

1. There are several places in this section where the narrative

employs irony to point up discrepancies between what characters do and say, and what their private agendas may be. Look for such sections and consider how they work, and what their effect is on your attitudes.

2. What is the function of allusions to other works of art (novels, paintings) as they are employed in this section?

3. Analyse the theme of moral responsibility as it unfolds in Part Three. How does the consideration of this theme relate to the overall treatment of the question in the book as a whole?

4. The pace of the novel begins to speed up as events unfold. How is this change achieved, and how does it compare, say, with the pace of the opening of Part One?

PART FOUR. 1943.
CHAPTER I (pp. 383–400)

Focus on: time and narrative structure

CRITICALLY EVALUATE . . .
— The first three sections of this chapter are set out in reverse order in relation to the 'real' time sequence. That is, we begin in the early morning with Charlotte and Sylvie Cariteau deciding to move the Duguay boys (pp. 383–4); we go back to the night before when Charlotte arrives at the Cariteaus' having escaped from the German soldiers guarding her and Julien at the Domaine (pp. 384–5); and then we go further back to what happened to Julien after she had fled the Domaine (pp. 385–7). Why has Faulks chosen to present events in this order? What is the effect, in terms of pacing and dramatic impact?

Focus on: the theme of war and its effects

COMMENT ON AND IMAGINE . . .

— On p. 388 Charlotte says to Sylvie, 'I will come back.' Where have you heard these words before in the novel? What drives the characters to say them? Will she come back? Why do you think that they imagine they need to come back?

Focus on: the theme of fantasy and self-construction

INTERPRET AND EXPLAIN . . .

— Charlotte has invented – or rather has had invented for her by Faulks – many 'explanations' of how she sees herself or how she presents her concept of her own character to the world. Here is another on p. 391: 'This, it was suddenly clear to Charlotte, was her hope of salvation. She would endure the agony of having to abandon her search for Gregory if she could heal these harsh familial wounds.' How far has Charlotte's drive always been to 'heal . . . harsh familial wounds'? Whose wounds? Which family? Or families?

Focus on: your own response

CONSIDER . . .

— In the section on pp. 392–8 Julien confronts Benech. Ask yourself how you feel about the events narrated here. Then ask yourself how the narrative method has contributed to making you feel the way you do.

Focus on: characterisation

RETELL . . .

— Nancy Brogan reappears here (pp. 399–400). Tell her story of this scene in her own words. Then work out what information you are given in Faulks's third-person narration that allows for her character to be so clearly portrayed in such a small space.

PART FOUR
CHAPTER 2 (pp. 401–14)

Focus on: language, vocabulary and imagery

CRITICALLY EVALUATE . . .
— Read p. 401. There are a number of images here to do with the mouth, with breathing, with speaking, with being able to express oneself. Count up as many as you can find. (They will be of many different kinds. Try to distinguish them thematically, linguistically and in terms of metaphor.) Then assess how this build-up works on you as the reader, and how the writer is orchestrating your reaction and point of view. (Note: if you are an older reader who lived through the Second World War, then your reactions may be different from those of a younger reader who did not have that experience. Which are you? Be aware of your 'readerly' position before you begin this exercise.)

Focus on: connections, allusion and reference

TRACE AND COMMENT ON . . .
— Several themes begin to come together in this chapter. On p. 402 mention is made of the canvas that Charlotte packed for Levade. Then on pp. 405 and 409 the narrative tells us that Levade has begun to dream again. And on p. 403 and then on pp. 407–8 we met the 'head of the staircase', who is called Hartmann. Using the information you have acquired in the course of reading this novel, analyse the significance of the canvas and the dreams. If you have read Faulks's *The Girl at*

the Lion d'Or you will recognise Hartmann. What is the significance of these internal and external references?

PART FOUR
CHAPTER 3 (pp. 415-28)

Focus on: connections, allusion and reference

RESEARCH AND COMPARE . . .
— On pp. 416–17 a new character called Levi is introduced. Except that, for readers of Faulks's *Birdsong*, he is not a new character (Levi appears towards the end of that book). Consider how this overlapping of characters works. There are small hints in *Birdsong* of what is to come. Compare what you know of Levi and Hartmann, from the other novels in which they appear, with what you learn about them here.

EVALUATE . . .
— This chapter looks back to the past and the First World War, but it also looks forward to the future, a kind of version of 'now' when Charlotte and Julien will be middle-aged, or elderly. On p. 419 Charlotte imagines that future and how she will return to visit 'all the people who had so unquestioningly helped her'. Where have you heard this promise to return before? What do you think drives these characters to make that promise? Why does Charlotte want to imagine that future? And – especially – consider and evaluate the effect on the reader as this image of the future is conjured up. Why is it important that it comes here, towards the end of the novel?

Focus on: characterisation

DISCUSS . . .
— In the last section of this chapter (pp. 422–28) Charlotte

is staying alone in the hotel at Châteaudun and experiences a potentially difficult and threatening encounter with a German officer. But the early part of the passage concerns Charlotte's own thoughts about her character: the person she thinks she is; the way other people perceive her. How does the episode with the German underline and endorse the conclusions that Charlotte comes to about her own character?

PART FOUR
CHAPTER 4 (pp. 429–36)

Focus on: setting and atmosphere

CONTRAST . . .
— Though Paris is occupied by the German army, Charlotte still recognises the Paris she had known and loved before the war. Contrast the scenes set in Paris with the scenes in the holding camp at Drancy.

Focus on: race and discrimination

RESEARCH . . .
— On pp. 429–30 Charlotte gets into a train carriage on the Paris Metro that is reserved for Jews. Research other places and times where similar strategies of segregation have been employed or made law. You might try to find out about the race laws that existed during the twentieth century in places like South Africa or Rhodesia (as Zimbabwe was then known). Or else find out about the treatment of African–Americans in the southern states of America. Look up the name of Rosa Parks in a history book or on the internet. What can you discover about her 'act of resistance'? How do those examples relate to what happened to the Jews under the Third Reich?

And how do they relate to what happens in Faulks's fictional portrayal of those historical events?

PART FOUR
CHAPTER 5 (pp. 437–60)

Focus on: the theme of identity

CONSIDER . . .
— 'Some of the children swapped name tags' (p. 441). Consider the implications of this. In what ways is the erosion of identity played out in this section? Think about the ways in which identity and self-definition are important to moral issues and form the basis of many human rights.

RELATE, CONNECT AND EXPLAIN THE IMAGE . . .
— In the passage where Peter's last journey out of France is being planned there is mention of the suitcase that he will borrow from Nancy and return after the war. In the passage describing the children's journey, André loses (and then finds) Sylvie Cariteau's suitcase – the one he and Jacob had used for tobogganing down the stairs. What is the metaphorical significance of each of these two suitcases? What do cases suggest to you?

CONSIDER AND EVALUATE . . .
— André reads the messages scrawled on the wall (p. 449). A Jewish orderly brings the children postcards to write messages on and throw from the train (p. 450). Why do you think people leave messages in such circumstances? Can you think of any recent events where people, at an extreme moment, left just such messages? What would you do in this kind of situation? To whom would you want to send a message?

Focus on: reader response and knowledge

DEFINE . . .

— As the next consignment of Jews is collected to be despatched to the concentration camps, the narrative tells us that 'few of them believed the foul gossip of gas and crematoria' (p. 445). Consider what you know about these events. What effect does this statement have on you, in the light of your own knowledge of the historical events of the war years? How would you describe the literary character of this statement set against your own knowledge? Is it: ironic, pathetic, bathetic?

ASK YOURSELF . . .

— Why has Faulks chosen to present this last journey to the gas chambers (pp. 457–60) from the point of view of a child, and a group of children? What is the effect of this on your reactions?

Focus on: the theme of parents and children

COMMENT ON . . .

— Charlotte has made it her business to find Levade in order to explain Julien's actions and heal the rift that might have been made between them, if he continued to misunderstand why Julien did what he did. André longs for his parents. On p. 451 an unnamed Jewish woman looks for the last time at her child. On p. 455 Charlotte reads one of the letters that she has found, written by a father to his daughter. What are the connections between these various parent-and-child relations? Why are they being built up in this way at this particular point in the novel? How does this relate to the theme worked out in the novel as a whole, especially in relation to Charlotte and her father?

PART FOUR
CHAPTER 6 (pp. 461–84)

Focus on: language, vocabulary and setting

EXAMINE, RESEARCH AND ILLUSTRATE . . .

On p. 465 Mr Jackson quotes a war slogan: 'Is your journey really necessary?' This was a political slogan coined in 1939 to discourage civil servants from going home for Christmas. Other war slogans might include:

- 'Make do and mend', from the 1940s
- 'Careless talk costs lives', from the Second World War
- 'Dig for victory', coined in the Second World War to persuade anyone who had land to grow food
- 'Coughs and sneezes spread diseases. Trap the germs in your handkerchief', health advice during the Second World War
- '*Taisez-vous! Méfiez-vous! Les oreilles ennemies vous écoutent*': 'Keep your mouth shut! Be on your guard! Enemy ears are listening to you', an official notice posted in France in 1915.

— Can you find or think of any others? What is the purpose of such slogans? Obviously they give advice, but what makes them memorable? And do you think they work in achieving their objective? How far does Jackson's use of this phrase here contribute to the period flavour of the novel?

— On p. 466 Jackson says that Charlotte has 'caught us with our trousers down, if you'll forgive the expression'. How does this popular expression work? What does it mean: a. literally, and b. metaphorically? Why is it particularly appropriate in this context? And how has Faulks given new life to a 'dead metaphor'?

Focus on: characterisation

CONSIDER . . .

— Daisy says to Charlotte, 'You're a rum one, aren't you?' (p. 471). Look through this chapter to see how Charlotte's character is being presented now. Where else have you encountered moments when other characters have puzzled over, or been surprised by, the discrepancy between the way Charlotte looks and what she does? Look forward to what happens in this chapter in the sections on pp. 472–6 and 481–4. In the light of these events, and the shadow that Charlotte's obscure 'memory' has cast over the whole story, why is it important that we are asked to contemplate Charlotte's new strengths at this point in the novel?

Focus on: connections, and the theme of parents and children

LIST AND COMPARE . . .

— Two long-withheld secrets are about to be revealed: the first is what really happened to William Gray and his company of men when they had charge of a group of German prisoners of war; the second is what happened – in so far as it is explained at all – between Charlotte and her father, when she was a child and he had just returned from the war. List all the occasions in this section where relations between parents and children are mentioned. Compare their different situations with Charlotte's and William Gray's.

RESEARCH AND REWRITE . . .

— William Gray appears in Faulks's *Birdsong*, both where he encounters Stephen Wraysford at the Front and in the sections of the novel set much later, when Stephen's granddaughter Elizabeth seeks out men who knew her grandfather as she tries to understand who he was and what he suffered during the

141

First World War. Take what you know of William Gray's life from *Birdsong* and *Charlotte Gray* and retell this story in your own words. Remember that you will end up with pieces of the jigsaw that date from 1918, 1942–3 and the 1970s.

EXPLAIN . . .

— 'For the first time he believed that his own life, however tarnished in his eyes, was what was necessary for the redemption of hers' (p. 479). 'She felt the return of Gregory had a bearing on her father, too, and that there might yet be some way out of their impasse' (p. 479). Though there is no obvious connection between Charlotte's reunion with Gregory and her imminent reconciliation with her father, this linking has been made into a major theme through the book. Find the places where this metaphorical connection is made, and then consider how the following three things might be related to each other: Charlotte's relationship with her father; her belief in her passion for Gregory; and the development of Charlotte's character across the novel as a whole.

PART FOUR
CHAPTER 7 (pp. 485–90)

Focus on: resolutions and narrative method

DEFINE . . .

— In this chapter many stories are resolved, often by taking us back to something, someone or some scene that we have already seen in the novel. Look for as many of these as you can find and define the relevance of each to Charlotte's story. (Some examples would include: Daisy's flat, Charlotte's old room, Robin Morris, Dr Wolf.) In what ways is this neat tying up of narrative ends contradicted by William Gray's warning that 'it was dangerous ever to think that one had solved buried problems of memory and fear. The human desire for neatness, he said, would always ultimately be defeated by the chaos of the mind's own truths' (p. 486)?

PART FOUR
CHAPTER 8 (pp. 491–6)

Focus on: endings and atmosphere

ASK YOURSELF . . .

— Is this a happy ending? Are you satisfied by it? If not, why not? If yes, why? How does Faulks create the atmosphere of 'slightly frantic joy' that Charlotte experiences?

READ CLOSELY AND CONSIDER . . .

— Look at the passage on pp. 495–6:

> In Charlotte's mind, Gregory belonged to the category of dreams and traumas. The possibility of happiness he had once held out, and that she had briefly tasted, was of an intensity so great that even at the time it had already seemed to belong to the past. The power of such feelings, it seemed to her, lay in their promise of transcendence. People followed them and believed in them because they offered not only a paradise of sensation but the promise of meaning, too; like the miracle of art, they held out an explanation of all the other faltering lights by which people were more momentarily guided.

— In what ways might this conclusion be read as a summary of the novel as a whole?

CRITICALLY EVALUATE . . .

— The last word of this chapter – and of the novel – is 'disappeared'. If you look back at the end of Chapter 5 in Part Four (p. 460) you will see that the last word there is also 'disappeared'. What is the effect of these two very different endings – for André and Jacob, and for Charlotte and Peter – being linked by this word? Now make a detailed comparison of these two last paragraphs. You will see that they both contain a number of the same words. Critically evaluate the ironic effect of this, and the implications of the thematic connection.

PART FOUR

Looking over Part Four

QUESTIONS FOR DISCUSSION OR ESSAYS

1.   Consider the theme of redemption in Part Four and in the novel as a whole.

2.   Discuss the portrayal of and the theme of 'the memory of war' in *Charlotte Gray*.

3.   'In Charlotte's mind, Gregory belonged to the category of dreams and traumas.' Examine the roles played by 'dreams and traumas' in this section and in the novel as a whole.

4.   Does *Charlotte Gray* offer a happy ending?

5.   Trace the narrative techniques of allusion and reference and the parallels used by Faulks in this novel (and in his others, if you have read them).

Looking back over the whole novel

QUESTIONS FOR DISCUSSION OR ESSAYS

1. Consider the treatment of memory in *Charlotte Gray*.

2. 'History is already being re-written' (p. 492). How does Faulks use history and the theme of the rewriting of history in *Charlotte Gray*?

3. Some critics have complained that because Peter Gregory is absent for so much of the story, his characterisation is 'thin'. Can you make a case for the significance of his absence in relation to the characterisation of Charlotte?

4. Why is *Charlotte Gray* the right title for this novel?

5. There are a great number of train journeys in *Charlotte Gray*. Take the descriptions of any two or three of these journeys and consider how they relate to the themes of the novel as a whole.

6. 'In times of war men act, women wait.' Comment on this statement in the light of what happens in *Charlotte Gray*.

7. 'What is present can't be imagined, and imagination is the only faculty we have for apprehending beauty' (p. 295). Analyse the relevance of this saying of Levade's in relation to the novel as a whole.

8. Describe and evaluate the period setting and the language of *Charlotte Gray*.

9. Define and assess the ways in which Faulks has used the

events of the deportation of the Jews from Occupied territory in France in the 1940s.

10. Examine the theme of parents and children in *Charlotte Gray*.

Contexts, comparisons and complementary readings

CHARLOTTE GRAY

Focus on: the theme of war and women's experience of war

EVALUATE . . .

— Read *The Diary of Anne Frank*, which was first published by her father in 1947 as *The Diary of a Young Girl*. Anne was a teenager when the Nazis occupied Holland. Because her family was Jewish, its members were required to wear the yellow Star of David. When they realised how many Jews were being deported, some non-Jewish friends arranged for the Franks and another family to go into hiding in the 'Annexe', the back section of a house in Amsterdam that was not visible from the street, and the entrance to which was concealed behind a bookcase. While living there, Anne kept a diary. The family was eventually discovered and deported, and Anne died in Belsen concentration camp. Only her father survived, and he discovered the diary on his return to the Annexe some years later. Use this comparison to think about Faulks's themes.

— Read Jerrard Tickell's *Odette: the story of a British agent* (1949). This is the true story of Odette Churchill, who was an English spy in France assisting the resistance during the Second World War. How do Charlotte's experiences compare with those described by Odette?

— Read David Hare's play *Plenty* (1973). It is about an English woman who assists the resistance in France. It is also about her life after the war. Consider which scenes in this play might be compared with scenes in *Charlotte Gray*. Why has Hare chosen to present the scenes of the play *not* in chronological order? In what ways does this compare with Faulks's narrative method and his occasional intermeshing of different, non-chronologically arranged scenes? What effect does this have on the reader of play or novel?

Characterisation

ANALYSE . . .

— There is a film version of Faulks's *Charlotte Gray* starring Cate Blanchett, directed by Gillian Armstrong, and released in 2002. If you can see the film, consider how Charlotte's character is built up there. What clues from the novel have been used to contribute to the depiction of Charlotte's character? How convincing do you find her in each version?

— Read Faulks's *The Fatal Englishman* (1996). How do the true stories here compare with the fictional story of Peter Gregory?

LOOK BACK . . .

— Here you will find the answers to the test that we offered you in the reading activities for Part One, Chapter 9. Look at the interpretations given below: they define the priorities in your life.

- Cow signifies CAREER
- Tiger signifies PRIDE
- Sheep signifies LOVE
- Horse signifies FAMILY
- Pig signifies MONEY
- Your description of a dog implies YOUR OWN PERSONALITY
- Your description of a cat implies the PERSONALITY OF YOUR PARTNER
- Your description of a rat implies the PERSONALITY OF YOUR ENEMIES
- Your description of coffee is how you interpret SEX
- Your description of the sea implies YOUR OWN LIFE
- Yellow: someone you will never forget
- Orange: someone you consider your true friend
- Red: someone whom you really love
- White: your twin soul
- Green: someone you will remember for the rest of your life

The theme of memory and history

STUDY . . .

— Read Robert Gildea's *Marianne in Chains: In Search of the German Occupation, 1940–1945* (2002). How does this factual account of the Occupation of France help to give a perspective on the events of Faulks's fictional story in *Charlotte Gray*?

— In 1996 Binjamin Wilkomirski published a book called *Fragments*, which purported to be the true account of his life as a child in the concentration camps. The book won many prizes, but Wilkomirski's story was later revealed to have been untrue. He had in fact grown up as the adopted child of a well-off Swiss family. The book was withdrawn and he was described as someone suffering from so-called 'false memory

149

syndrome'. You can read about the events surrounding his exposure in Blake Eskin's *A Life in Pieces: The Making of Binjamin Wilkomirski* (2001). Consider the following questions. Does it matter that Wilkomirski's story was not true, if the work had literary value? How does the problem of 'false memory syndrome' work itself out in *Charlotte Gray*? What are the metaphorical connections between Charlotte's private trauma and the collective trauma suffered by Europe as history comes to terms with the events of the Second World War?

Other books that you might find helpful on this are Gitta Sereny's *The German Trauma: Experiences and Reflections 1938–2001* (2001) and Lawrence Norfolk's *In the Shape of a Boar* (2000). The latter is a fiction about memories and mis-memories of the Second World War as they are told in a fictional bestselling book which is partly a reference to Wilkomirski. A word of warning: if you do tackle the Norfolk account, the opening is tough – but persevere, because there is a point that will become clear, and it is important.

History, race, ethnic labelling

COMPARE AND CONTRAST . . .

— It is easy enough to imagine that the deportation, incarceration and execution of the Jews could never happen again – even though those events occurred only in the recent past. Read this leader taken from *The Times* on 23 May 2001, and consider the treatment of Hindus in Afghanistan as compared to that of the Jews in Nazi Germany.

> '*Badge of Shame: Afghanistan is going down the Nazi path of intolerance*'
> The edict by Muhammad Wali, the Taleban religious police minister, forcing Hindus in Afghanistan to wear

labels on their clothing to distinguish them from
Muslims is repulsive and also revealing. Anyone with
more sense of history than the blinkered and self-
righteous Islamic extremists ruling Kabul would see
the awful echoes of the Nazi decree forcing Jews to
wear a yellow Star of David. Little wonder that not
only Europe and America have reacted with horror;
India swiftly denounced the proposal as deplorable
and patent discrimination against minorities.

It is more than that. It is a clear indication that
Taleban zealotry is moving down the same mur-
derous and intolerant path as National Socialism.
Like the Nazis, the group that swept to power with
the pledge of ending the corruption and mismanage-
ment of the warlords now maintains itself in power
by intimidation. Its extremism, masking as religious
fervour, was directed first at its political enemies,
then at women and all those suspected of ideological
opposition, and now is turned on the most vulnerable group of all, the beleaguered non-Muslims. The
Taleban has already had its *Kristallnacht*, smashing the
religious symbols and historical artefacts of its perceived enemies; now it has passed its Nuremberg
Laws, institutionalising discrimination.

Luckily, there are few minorities left in
Afghanistan to suffer such humiliation. Most Hindus
have fled, and there are not many Christians or Jews
in Afghan cities. The Taleban leadership maintains
that its proposed fatwa on dress will guarantee the
protection of minorities. But far from recognising
different religious practices, the edict will force
Hindu women to veil themselves like Muslims. In
fact, it is another sign that as conditions in the
country deteriorate, hardliners are taking ever more

extreme positions to deflect blame, to cow a desperate population and take advantage of political divisions.

Drought has brought much of Afghanistan to the brink of starvation, and refugees are pouring into Pakistan. Much of the turmoil is Taleban-made, however. The ban on women working has left thousands of war widows imprisoned in their homes; the closure last week of the bakery funded by the United Nations has cut off one of the few outlets for subsidised bread; and the storming of the new 120-bed hospital by the religious police has shut one of the few places where victims of 21 years of war could seek treatment.

The hardening of the Taleban stance is dictated largely by the regime's near-total isolation. UN sanctions are hurting, but pride and paranoia have sabotaged any attempt to extradite the Saudi terrorist Osama bin Laden or to get peace talks going. Taleban policy is to boycott the UN, step up the ideological war and prepare the population for a new spring offensive against the Northern Alliance that still has a toehold in the north-west. Containment has become the only viable policy to deal with this loathsome regime; but, as with Nazi Germany, that offers little protection to the minorities within its borders.

— You may have heard of the novel by Thomas Keneally called *Schindler's Ark* (1982), which was made into a film entitled *Schindler's List*. It was based on a true story. Read this article taken from *The Times* on 27 April 2001. Consider how Faulks's themes of the way in which the past influences the present are represented by this true story.

'Widow fights to retrieve Schindler's original list'

The original list of 1,200 Jews rescued by Oskar Schindler during the Second World War was at the centre of a lawsuit in Stuttgart yesterday instigated by the German industrialist's widow.

Two years ago, hundreds of letters, photographs and certificates belonging to the Jews he saved from the gas chambers were found in a suitcase in an attic in Baden-Württemburg.

The story of the businessman who courted the SS after Germany invaded Poland and saved about 1,200 Jews by employing them in his factory was retold in a book and the film *Schindler's List*.

Now 93 and living in Argentina, Schindler's widow, Emilie, is claiming the papers and seeking £33,000 damages from the local newspaper which held them and passed them to the Yad Vashem Holocaust museum in Israel.

Yesterday the copyright case she initiated last year formally began in Stuttgart.

The suitcase was found in the loft of Schindler's last girlfriend's home in Hildesheim — stowed there in 1974 after he died. The couple who found the suitcase and original list of Jewish employees took it to the *Stuttgarter Zeitung* newspaper. There followed six articles and the documents were copied for the German Federal Archive before the originals were sent to Israel.

Frau Schindler's contention is that as the last living relative and heir, she has the copyright to the suitcase's contents.

A temporary restraining order was issued by a local court against the newspaper and its offices were searched last November. But it was too late as the suitcase and its contents were on the way to Israel. The newspaper struck back by obtaining a judgment to overturn the restraining order and billed the widow for its legal costs. It sent her copies of the original list but that did not placate her.

The main reason for her fury seems to be a thwarted book deal. Frau Schindler was signed up with a publisher in Munich for her biography, which would have been far more marketable had it been able to reveal the original list.

The case, in the District Court in Stuttgart, promises to be a dry affair and could last at least two years.

Communication and understanding

— If you look at the interview with Faulks, you will see that he refers (jokingly) to reading 'too much' Thomas Hardy, in relation to a question that we ask about letters going astray and the consequences for communication between people. Read Thomas Hardy's *Tess of the D'Urbervilles* (1891). Look especially at the chapter where Tess delivers a letter explaining her past to Angel Clare. How does what happens to that letter (he doesn't get it) compare with what happens to letters (lost, misdirected, not sent, even unwritten) in either Faulks's *Birdsong* or his *Charlotte Gray*?

VINTAGE
LIVING
TEXTS

The Girl at the
Lion d'Or

IN CLOSE-UP

Reading guides

THE GIRL AT THE LION D'OR

BEFORE YOU BEGIN TO READ
— Look at the interview with Faulks. You will see there that he identifies a number of recurring themes in his books, including:

- How the past affects and influences the present
- War and its effects
- Memory
- Redemption.

Other themes that you might like to consider include:

- The image of rural France
- Romance
- The portrayal of place
- Guilt and responsibility

Reading activities: detailed analysis

PART ONE
CHAPTERS 1 and 2 (pp. 11–24)

Focus on: place

LIST AND ANALYSE . . .

— Faulks says in the interview that developing the setting of his novels is one of the important aspects of his writing process. Look over these two chapters and note down the ways in which he describes the various places that we are introduced to here, including: the railway station at Janvilliers, the entrance to the hotel, Anne's bedroom, the bathroom and the linen closet, and the bar in the hotel. What are the specific details that make up the picture of a particular time and place?

Focus on: the voyeur and the role of the reader

EXPLAIN AND JUSTIFY . . .

— Roland spies on Anne in the very first chapter of this novel. He attempts to scrutinise her with his 'questing eye'. Consider the implications of this opening scene. Can you suggest *literary* reasons for including it? Do you feel in any way uncomfortable about it? In what ways are we, as readers, put into a similar position along with Roland, as we spy on Anne through the omniscient view of the narrator?

PART ONE
CHAPTER 3 (pp. 25–30)

Focus on: parallel lives

EVALUATE . . .

— We have already learned that Anne has some mysterious past, which means that she uses a name that is not her own. Now we are introduced to Hartmann for the first time – though we have heard his character discussed in Chapter 2. When Anne looks at Hartmann playing tennis, she seems to see 'the ghost of his vulnerable boyhood'. Consider the effects of these links set up between Anne and Hartmann and their respective pasts. What are you being made to feel might happen?

PART ONE
CHAPTER 4 and 5 (pp. 31–49)

Focus on: sense of place

COMPARE . . .

— In the interview Faulks says that 'houses really really get me going'. The house in *The Girl at the Lion d'Or* is based on a real place, as is the Domaine in *Charlotte Gray*. Read the interview, and then compare the descriptions of the two houses in the two novels.

Focus on: characterisation

SUMMARISE . . .
— In these chapters Hartmann is introduced, as is his wife Christine. Write a short description of each of them, based on the information you are given here. Then ask yourself these two questions about each one: 'What is their key characteristic?' and 'What is their defining life experience?'

Focus on: plot

INTERPRET . . .
— At the end of these two chapters Anne has suggested to Hartmann that she should come to work at the Manor, and he has agreed to see her in order to consider it. When she falls asleep, 'she dreamed that she had known him as a child and had enlisted his help to stop her life from changing' (p. 49). What do you think is going to happen? What in the method of setting out plot and narrative makes you think that?

PART ONE
CHAPTER 6 (pp. 50–64)

Focus on: the themes of war and how the past influences the present

DEFINE . . .
— Anne and Hartmann discuss the political situation and the growing tension between public political events and private lives. This novel is set in 1936. At the same time Anne has developed eczema – which, though not unconnected to the kinds of work she has to do, seems to have something to do with her past and her personality. And Hartmann tells her about

his background and about his books. How are the personal
and the political overlapped in the scenes in this chapter? If
you have read Faulks's *Birdsong* and/or *Charlotte Gray*, consider
how these themes of war and the past influencing the present
are connected in relation to the character of Hartmann as he
appears in those other two novels.

Focus on: allusion and reference

RESEARCH AND COMPARE . . .
— On p. 64 Anne picks up one of Hartmann's books and
ask him what it is about. The book is *The Story of Troilus and
Cressida*, and Hartmann says that it is a 'love story'. There are
several versions of this story, which takes place during the siege
of Troy when the Greek armies were trying to take back Helen,
who had been abducted by Paris, the son of Priam, King of
Troy. Look up this story: read about it in a *Dictionary of Classical
Mythology*, or read Robert Graves's version of the Greek myths
(1955) or the relevant section in a translation of Homer's *The
Iliad* (8th century BC). Alternatively, you could read Chaucer's
version in *Troilus and Criseyde* (*c.* 1385) or Shakespeare's play
Troilus and Cressida (*c.* 1602). The story is not always the same,
but compare whichever version you choose with what is happening in Faulks's novel. In what ways is this particular story
an appropriate clue to what has happened – and will happen
– to Anne and Hartmann's relationship?

PART ONE
CHAPTER 7 (pp. 65–74)

Focus on: characterisation

EVALUATE . . .
— In Part One, Chapter 6 Hartmann called Anne 'robust', and – in order to control her emotions – she said to herself, 'Perhaps, then, I had better be' (p. 64). How is Anne's character further developed in this chapter? In what ways is she 'robust'? In what ways is she vulnerable?

COMPARE . . .
— If you have read Faulks's *Charlotte Gray* you might consider the ways in which the character of Charlotte is developed in a similar way to the character of Anne, as it is portrayed in the novel as a whole. Some elements that you could think about might include: the relationship between father and daughter; the presence of a half-remembered trauma; the war setting; the way other characters in the two novels perceive the two girls; their attitudes to their lovers; their growth to independence.

PART ONE

Looking over Part One

QUESTIONS FOR DISCUSSION OR ESSAYS
1. Discuss how the period setting and atmosphere are created in Part One.

2. How is the character of Anne developed in this part?

3. Consider the significance of 'home' in Part One.

PART TWO
CHAPTER 1 (pp. 77–81)

Focus on: the image of the voyeur

COMPARE . . .

— On p. 79 Anne tells Hartmann how she has always felt observed in the bathroom at the hotel. We know that she is not imagining this. Compare her account of this feeling with the narrative account of what actually happened in Chapter 1 of Part One. What is the significance of Anne telling Hartmann about this feeling, just at the time when she is also telling him about her life at the hotel and her sense of the unjust way in which she has been treated?

PART TWO
CHAPTERS 2 and 3 (pp. 82–91)

Focus on: the theme of desire

TRACE . . .

— Hartmann thinks about sexual desire and his own attitudes to it, and how they were deeply affected and changed by the way in which his experience during the First World War showed him mangled and mutilated bodies. Consider the account here of the fluctuations of desire – in the broadest sense – in each of the three characters portrayed in these two chapters: that is, Hartmann, Christine and Anne. In what ways are their attitudes the same and in what ways are they different? In particular, how do the two women think about sex and desire, in comparison with the way Hartmann thinks?

Focus on: the theme of looking

COMPARE AND INVENT . . .
— Hartmann looks at the naked body of his wife (p. 85) and suddenly sees a new perspective. This comes just after Anne has told Hartmann about her feeling of being looked at, and just before Hartmann gives Christine a pair of binoculars to look at the birds. What connections can you create between these parallel forms of 'looking'?

PART TWO
CHAPTERS 4, 5 and 6 (pp. 92–117)

Focus on: the theme of home

RETELL . . .
— Look at each of the passages and episodes that describe the rooms Hartmann has rented for Anne at Mlle Calmette's. Write an account, from Anne's point of view, of what is in the rooms. What does she treasure about the place that is actually concerned with things and objects? What more than that do the rooms mean to her? Can you begin to suggest why, from the hints about her past that we have been given so far? Remember too that this is a novel, so the names that characters are given are contrived. What is the significance of Mlle Calmette's name?

Focus on: the theme of men and women

CRITICALLY EVALUATE . . .
Hartmann, thinking that he does not want Anne to spend too much money, suggests that she cook *coq au vin* for their planned supper. As we discover, Anne does not have the practical facil-

ities for preparing this particular dish, which is designed for an older, tougher chicken and needs long cooking in a slow oven. All she has is a single gas ring, so she had to keep looking at the dish and checking that the liquid does not boil away. Hartmann, being a man – so the implication is – has not thought of this.

— In what ways – in the novel as a whole – does Sebastian Faulks develop the differences in attitude and expectation between men and women? Are these differences particular to a specific historical moment, or might they be relevant in all situations? To think about this problem you might like to read a popular book on the subject, such as John Gray's *Men Are from Mars, Women Are from Venus: A Practical Guide for Improving Communication and Getting What You Want in Your Relationships* (1993).

— Alternatively, look at the following examples of the differences between men's and women's vocabulary and what they mean. They come from an article by Allison Pearson published in the *Evening Standard* on 3 October 2001. Some of them are her own, while others she has collected from 'the store of wisdom on the internet', so this is not just a personal view, but one that is more general.

'*Women's vocabulary*'

Fine: this is the word we use at the end of any argument when we know we are in the right, but need to shut you up. As a man, you should *never* use 'fine' to describe how a woman looks. This will cause you to have one of those arguments.

Five minutes: this is half an hour. It is equivalent to the five minutes that your football game is going to last before you take out the rubbish.

Nothing: this means something and you should be on your guard. 'Nothing' usually signifies an argument that will last 'five minutes' and end with the word 'fine'.

A loud sigh: this means the woman thinks you are an idiot and wonders why she is wasting her time standing here and arguing with you over 'nothing'.

A soft sigh: 'soft sighs' are one of the few things that men actually understand. She is content. Your best bet is to not move or breathe and she will stay that way.

Oh: this word followed by any statement spells trouble. Example: 'Oh, don't worry.' If she says, 'Oh' before a statement, run – do not walk – to the nearest exit. She will tell you that she is 'fine', but do not expect her to talk to you for at least two days.

Thanks: a woman is thanking you. Do not faint, just say you're welcome.

Thanks a lot: not to be confused with 'Thanks'. A woman will say 'thanks a lot' when she is really pissed off with you. It indicates that you have behaved in a callous way, and will be followed by the 'loud sigh'. Be careful not to ask what is wrong after the 'loud sigh', as she will only tell you 'nothing'.

'Men's vocabulary'

What's wrong? This may look like an enquiry, but actually requires no answer and certainly not one containing any kind of complaint. The male will feel he has done his bit simply by registering that the woman may be less than 100 per cent content. If she indicates that this is indeed the case, she risks being labelled 'difficult'. See also: Moody, Mad and Is It That Time of the Month Again?

What's wrong now? As above, but with the impli-cation of the woman's puzzling, indeed stubborn inability to be pleased with his excellent conduct. The best reply to this is 'nothing', which may usefully be garnished with a deep sigh.

I'm here, aren't I? A declaration of love. It's important to remember that men are really quite simple organisms, equipped to go out and track bison, bring them home and burn them on the barbecue. Anything you require which is outside the basic template of hunting and providing – love, tact, birthday presents, etc – is genuinely puzzling to them. See also: But I Thought We Were Having A Good Time.

I picked up your dry cleaning, didn't I? A standard response when you point out that you do 'absolutely everything'! There is no point snorting derisively. Men, like puppies, can only be brought on by a careful, balanced regime of firmness and praise. Try to avoid a reply that puts them in the wrong, mainly because they simply won't go there.

You're mad: A phrase used to denote any behaviour that distinguishes the woman from a sexually available vacuum cleaner.

Focus on: convention and characterisation

EXPLAIN . . .

— At the end of Chapter 5 (p. 111) Hartmann encourages Anne to ask for a few days' holiday from the hotel. He says, 'Go on, Anne. You're a brave girl. "Robust" – wasn't that the word I used?' He refers back to an earlier episode, but Anne is indeed becoming braver and more robust, especially in relation to coping with the innuendo and suspicion over her position with Hartmann, in view of his having taken these rooms for her. Trace the reactions of the other characters to Anne's decision to move from the hotel, and explain how her character is being developed as she deals with their reactions.

Focus on: war and the memory of war

ACCOUNT FOR . . .

— In Anne's brief meeting with the Patron we are given a swift account of his memories of the First World War and his reaction to it in later life. Remember that the events of the war took place in 1914–18. It is now 1936. Can you account for the Patron's extreme reaction?

PART TWO
CHAPTER 7 (pp. 118–58)

Focus on: narrative structure and plot

RELATE . . .

— In the course of this long chapter Anne and Hartmann go away together to stay with his friend Etienne Beauvais, and Anne and Charles become lovers. Then – at the hotel where they stay after Charles's car breaks down – Anne tells him the story of her childhood and the trauma that haunts her. Why has Faulks put these two episodes together? How do they reflect and compare with each other?

Focus on: the theme of home

ACCOUNT FOR . . .

— Look at the various descriptions of Anne and Charles's lodgings in the granary during their stay at Merlaut. How does Faulks build the specifics of the setting? And why is this room so important to Anne? How does it relate to her attitudes to her rooms at Mlle Calmette's?

168

Focus on: the theme of war and the memory of war

RELATE . . .
— Anne's story of what happened to her father comes after we have heard the story of what happened to the Patron of the Lion d'Or during the First World War. How do these two personal tragedies relate to one another? What themes and criticisms do they present of the prevailing mood during war?

PART TWO

Looking over Part Two

QUESTIONS FOR DISCUSSION OR ESSAYS
1. Consider the portrayal and significance of memory in Part Two.

2. Compare and contrast Christine's character with that of Anne.

3. Analyse the treatment of desire in this section.

PART THREE
CHAPTER I (pp. 161–4)

Focus on: sympathy and point of view

CONSIDER . . .
— Hartmann now contemplates the story Anne has told him about her past. How are your attitudes to this story altered by your being given his perspective on it? Towards the end of the chapter Hartmann compares his reaction to Anne's story with the peculiar and sudden 'odd rush of unexplained compassion'

that he had felt when he was talking to Roussel about the building works at the Manor. What symbolic significance is there in this connection in Hartmann's mind? How might his sympathy for Anne's past – a past forced on her by the external circumstances of the war – connect to his sympathy for Roussel, whose present circumstances, as we will learn, are related to the plight of France in the aftermath of the war?

PART THREE
CHAPTERS 2 and 3 (pp. 165–92)

Focus on: parallel lives

COMPARE AND CONTRAST . . .
— Anne goes about her work in the hotel. Charles and his friend Antoine discuss the political situation; Mattlin decides to seek out a new mistress; Christine hears strange noises and sees strange cracks in the walls of the Manor. Compare and contrast these parallel scenes. What is the effect of their being presented in this overlapping narrative structure?

Focus on: the theme of public morality and private behaviour

COMPARE, CONTRAST AND JUDGE . . .
— When Antoine and Hartmann go to see the minister he tells them the story of his holiday in Corsica and what happened there – events that have been revealed, and which seem to be leading towards his disgrace (pp. 179–82). Consider the minister's circumstances in relation to Hartmann's position with Anne. Compare the moral responsibility of each man in relation to their public presentation of themselves and their private behaviour. Now think back to Roland and his spying on

Anne – and the other girls at the Lion d'Or. Are there any qualitative differences between the actions of the three men? How would you rank their behaviour in terms of 'crime' or culpability? Can any one of the three men be justified in what they are doing? If so, why?

PART THREE
CHAPTERS 4 and 5 (pp. 193–219)

Focus on: narrative connections

ANALYSE WITH A CLOSE READING . . .

— Look carefully at the opening sentences of each of the five sections of Chapter 4, on pp. 193, 196, 198, 202 and 206. The autumn has arrived with a change in the weather, but events in the private lives of the characters in this novel are also beginning to go cold and break down. By analysing the vocabulary of each of these opening sentences, and listing the words that convey tension, physical discomfort and a miserable mood, consider how Faulks is building up images of rupture and pain.

— Then look through Chapter 5 and carry out the same exercise. Consider especially the opening lines of Chapter 5: 'In the middle of the night Hartmann was awoken by what sounded like a pistol shot' (p. 208). What – given the date of 1936, and the theme of war played out in *The Girl at the Lion d'Or* – is the significance of the two phrases 'in the middle of the night' and 'like a pistol shot'?

CRITICALLY EVALUATE . . .

— At the end of Chapter 5 Anne returns to the hotel and sees a woman at the window, whom she recognises as Madame Bouin. The narrative point of view then switches to Madame

Bouin's perspective for the first and only time in the novel. Hitherto we have only seen her through Anne's eyes and through the eyes of the other workers in the hotel, who regard her as an unfeeling tartar. Why has Faulks introduced her at this point in the novel? What connections can you make between her story, Anne's story of her past and the Patron's story?

LIST AND CONSIDER . . .

— On p. 219, at the end of the section dealing with Madame Bouin, there are a lot of numbers. Write them all down. Why are they here? What narrative strategies does this device of naming numbers achieve?

PART THREE
CHAPTER 6 (pp. 220–28)

Focus on: plot structure

EXAMINE . . .

— On pp. 221–22 Hartmann runs into the Patron of the hotel. This is the second (and last) time that he will appear. Look back at the section where we last met him, when Anne went to ask for leave from her work. What does it suggest, in terms of the plotting and themes of the novel, that he should reappear now?

— On p. 221 Hartmann and the Patron discuss the headline 'SALENGRO CLEARED'. On pp. 224–5 another newspaper report tells of his suicide. Again, we have already met Salengro and now he reappears – like the Patron – at this point in the story. What metaphorical and moral connections are being made by these repetitions?

— Now look at the last section of the chapter on pp. 227–8.

How have these events affected Hartmann? How might they be contributing to his present state of feeling, to his attitude to Anne and his own sense of moral responsibility, and to his coming to a decision that dictates what he is about to do?

PART THREE
CHAPTER 7 (pp. 229-34)

Focus on: the theme of moral responsibility

IMAGINE AND EVALUATE . . .
— What do you think of what happens in this chapter? How do you feel about it? Has Hartmann acted correctly? Honourably? Kindly? To whom do you think he owes his first duty? Christine? Anne? Himself? Society? If you are in a group, get someone to take Anne's side in the episode and someone else to take Hartmann's, then play out the arguments. How does this very private scene relate to the larger public events – both past and present – that have provided the background to the novel as a whole?

Focus on: narrative patterns and imagery

OUTLINE . . .
— Link the events of this chapter and the encounter between Anne and Hartmann with:

● The crumbling of Hartmann's house
● The dream that Anne had on p. 127
● The story of Anne's father.

— What patterns are being brought out by these comparisons?

PART THREE
CHAPTERS 8 and 9 (pp. 235–42)

Focus on: parallel lives and characterisation

DESCRIBE . . .

— Anne's immediate reaction to Hartmann's dismissal of her is set against his. Look over these two chapters and write down twenty key words that describe how each of these two characters is feeling and the kinds of people they are. When you have found twenty words for each, put them in order of priority, so that you end up with a hierarchical description of both Hartmann's and Anne's key characteristics.

Focus on: motives and moral responsibility

JUSTIFY . . .

— On p. 240 the narrative tells us that Hartmann acted not through cruelty, but 'through an excess of sympathy'. What is there in the novel as a whole that justifies this explanation? Try to spell out public and private motives that might make Hartmann's choice the right one.

PART THREE
CHAPTER 10 (pp. 243–9)

Focus on: characterisation

DEFINE . . .

— What is it in the elements of Anne's character that you have learned in the course of reading this novel that explains her actions and decisions in this chapter? Remember that she has several times been described as 'robust'. Where is that robustness demonstrated now? How does the moment in the garden connect to, and in some ways end, her story?

Focus on: endings

RESEARCH AND COMPARE . . .

— If you have read Faulks's *Birdsong* and/or *Charlotte Gray*, then consider the endings of each of those novels. How do they differ from this novel's ending? In what ways might they be similar? *Charlotte Gray* has the most conventionally 'happy' ending; but is there any sense in which – 'happy' or 'unhappy' – these endings all convey the same message? About endurance? About redemption? About hope?

— In Faulks's novel *On Green Dolphin Street* the two lovers Frank and Mary part at the end. But we are teased by several possibilities of that not being the final outcome. Read the ending of that novel and consider how Faulks's endings have evolved – or not – over the years.

— When Hartmann and Anne looked at the books in his attic she asked him about *The Story of Troilus and Cressida* and wanted to know if it was a love story. Sebastian Faulks's *The Girl at the Lion d'Or* has been compared to two famous novels about love, passion, obsession and its discontents: Tolstoy's *Anna Karenina* (1873–7) and John Fowles's *The French Lieutenant's Woman* (1969). Read either or both of these books and consider how they might be compared to Faulks's novel.

— Fowles's *The French Lieutenant's Woman* famously offers a double ending: one is happy, and the couple are reunited; the other is unhappy, and their relationship is not resolved. Write yourself a happy ending for *The Girl at the Lion d'Or*. How convinced are you by your own alternative?

PART THREE

Looking over Part Three

QUESTIONS FOR DISCUSSION OR ESSAYS

1. Hartmann suffers from 'an excess of sympathy'. How is the question of personal sympathy related to public moral responsibility in the novel as a whole?

2. Consider the power of the past to affect the present.

3. Redemption is a favourite theme of Faulks. Analyse its presence and role in Part Three.

4. Discuss the different kinds of love presented in the novel as a whole.

Looking back over the whole novel

QUESTIONS FOR DISCUSSION OR ESSAYS

1. 'Louvet . . . had a theory that all unhappiness was a version of the same feeling' (pp. 11–12). Consider Louvet's proposition in relation to the various unhappinesses that Anne experiences in the course of the novel as a whole.

2. 'The house is undermined to create a cellar for old wines. So the house is France, making a shrine of the past and undermining the present and future.' Discuss.

3. The last words of the novel are '"Can I help?" he said.' Consider how this question illuminates the novel as a whole.

Contexts, Comparisons and Complementary Readings

THE GIRL AT LION D'OR

Focus on: the theme of trust and betrayal

COMPARE . . .

Read a translation of Pierre Choderlos de Laclos's novel *Les Liaisons Dangereuses* (1782), or read the dramatic adaptation of the novel by Christopher Hampton. The story of the novel and the play concerns the sexual mores of the late eighteenth century during the perod of the *ancien régime*. Like *The Girl at the Lion d'Or*, it is a story of seduction and betrayal. Compare the two texts. What difference does it make that Faulks's and Laclos's novels are set in very different historical periods? In particular, look at the scene where Valmont rejects his lover La Presidente de Tourvel, and compare it with the scene where Hartmann similarly and unexpectedly rejects Anne.

Focus on: the symbol of the house

RESEARCH . . .

Hartmann's manor house provides both setting and symbolic

value in Faulks's novel. Research other novels where the idea of the house takes on a figurative meaning which is more than just it being a house, providing shelter. You might look for novels that have the name of a house in the title, such as Jane Austen's *Mansfield Park* (1814), or Charles Dickens's *Bleak House* (1852–3). Or else, you might look at a novel such as Charlotte Brontë's *Jane Eyre* (1847), where the secrets of Thornfield Hall provide a major part of the plot. The same technique is used in Daphne du Maurier's novel *Rebecca* (1938), which is, in some senses, a rewriting of Brontë's *Jane Eyre*, with Max de Winter's ancestral home of Manderley standing in for Rochester's Thornfield Hall.

VINTAGE
LIVING
TEXTS

Reference

Selected extracts from reviews

These brief extracts from contemporary reviews of the novels are designed to be used to suggest angles on the text that may be relevant to the themes of the books, to their settings, their literary methods or their historical contexts, or to indicate their relevance to issues, questions or problems today.

Sometimes one reviewer's opinion will be entirely contradicted by another's. You might use these passages to ask yourself whether or not you agree with the writer's assessments. Or you might take phrases from these reviews to use in framing questions – for discussion, or for essays – about the texts.

The excerpts here have been chosen because they offer useful and intelligent observations. In general, though, when you are reading reviews in newspapers, it is best to remember two things: they are often written under pressure, and they have to give the reader some idea of what the book under discussion is like, so they tend to give space to summarising the plot.

None of these critical opinions are the last word. They are simply contributions to a cultural debate. As such, they should be approached with intellectual interest – because they can give the mood and tone of a particular time – and they should be treated with caution – because the very fact of that prevailing mood and time may intervene.

BIRDSONG

Alain de Botton, 22 August 1998
From the *Express*
On the popularity and appeal of *Birdsong*

Sebastian Faulks's *Birdsong* was published in 1993 and at once established itself as one of the most popular British novels in living memory. For the past five years, every train carriage seems to have had at least one passenger deeply engrossed in a copy, readers of the book often have conversations about what bits they like best (the sex scenes at the beginning and the First World War scenes in the middle tend to get the highest ratings, while the contemporary story at the end usually gets a thumbs down). *Birdsong* has to date sold close to half a million copies.

Ian Ousby, 11 September 1998
From the *Times Literary Supplement*
On the trilogy

Wherever you look these days, you find British novelists setting their work in France and British novelists looking back at the two World Wars that have disfigured this century. Sebastian Faulks is both kinds of novelist, and *Charlotte Gray* is his third novel to undertake both tasks at once. Set in a provincial French town in the 1930s, his first novel, *The Girl at the Lion d'Or*

(1989), lent its deliberately slight story resonance with oblique reminders of the political tensions which the coming war would aggravate rather than heal, as well as with oblique reminders of unhealed memories of the Great War. *Birdsong* (1993), by contrast, confronted the First World War with direct and self-conscious ambition, tackling the big issues and the big questions almost as bald-headedly as the Somme offensive which was the centrepiece of its narrative. Its very willingness to run the risk of cliché released a raw story-telling power that carried the book forward.

CHARLOTTE GRAY

Sean O'Brien, 22 August 1998
From the *Guardian*
On the portrayal of France and period detail

The greatest strength of Faulks's writing lies in description and evocation. His real and imagined French towns – Amiens, Janvilliers, Lavaurette – exert a dank, melancholy fascination. Their secrecy, tedium and inarticulate frustration seem almost paradisally complete. Their railway stations deliver people to fates none the less agonising for their banality. We know what people eat and what they smell like; their blend of indifference and despair at the succession of failed and undermined inter-war governments; the closeness to the surface of their Anti-Semitism; and we sense the swallowed misery of the millions of war-bereaved. Faulks also brings greater conviction to some of the French characters than to the British. Varieties of French collaboration with the Germans are the most interesting things in the book (and leave little doubt about how things would have gone if Hitler had successfully invaded Britain). Levade slowly shames the local gendarme into admitting his part in the deportation of a Jewish couple. Pichon, an official of Laval's government, deranged by legalism, justifies the intended arrest of Levade's father for his Jewish ancestry in a manner both farcical and chilling. The local schoolmaster Benech finds his *métier* with the pistol and black livery of the fascist Milice. The real life of *Charlotte Gray* is in these cameos.

Anita Brookner, 29 August 1998
From the *Spectator*
On the historical context

In this romantic, discursive, and sometimes bewildering account an important point is made: the war in France was less a war between the French and the Germans than a civil war, between the Milice and the undesirables, those who, when not actually Jewish, which would rule them out of the coming victory altogether, did not believe in the Hero of Verdun and his assurance that a greater France would soon sit with a greater Germany at Europe's top table. The English contribution to the resistance of such Frenchmen who retained a vestigial grasp of French honour was relatively frivolous: telephone messages to hairdressers and garage owners with exotic covers, supplies of food and weapons occasionally dropped by parachute, cryptic messages passed through unreliable networks. In comparison with their French counterparts, those very few heroes, the English contributed the sort of innocence compounded of ignorance and good will . . .

Beneath the fictitious events there is a reality which is partly unacknowledged. Thus the characters do not know, have not heard of what will become of Milice, though they do trust its architect, Laval, largely on account of his appearance. The Milice demands only a love of order, loyalty to Pétain, and hatred of Jews and communists. The Milice will recruit principally among malcontents, hooligans, and known trouble-makers who might otherwise be deported to Germany as part of Laval's eight-for-one exchange system for prisoners taken in the brief fight of May 1940, before capitulation. The law of 2 June 1941 gave the right of internment to the local prefecture of any Jews, foreign or French. Collaboration with the occupier was intended to safeguard the independence of a racially pure France. The names to remember in this context are those of Vallat, Darquier de Pellepoix, and Bousquet. Darquier de Pellepoix in particular believed that the Jewish crime was genetic and therefore ineradicable. In that sense, assimilated or invisible Jews were the most dangerous.

John Bayley, 1 September 1998
From the *Evening Standard*
On the historical context

As if conscientiously, he [Faulks] feels the need to bring in the fate of the Jewish children of Vichy France, deported to the transit centre at Drancy, from where they were shipped to Dachau and Auschwitz. This tale cannot but be moving, and it is powerfully and obliquely told. Faulks has a quiet feeling for human nature, and how, in extreme situations, it can call out the heroic or the base in the individual quite unpredictably.

His two boys helping each other on their way to disappearance in the gas chambers are memorably perceived and reminded me a little of *Love and War*, Leonid Grossman's great classic of Germany and Russia at war under their evil dictators. Grossman had seen it all, which is why his novel never appeared in Russia until recently.

Disappearance is Faulks's masterstroke, enlightening with mysterious potency the end of his novel. The word is two-faced. You can disappear into death, like the two little French boys, or into life, like Peter and Charlotte into the dark church 'heavy with the scent of cut flowers'. These two modes of disappearance end a novel which has grown in strength drawn from the conventions of a classic form.

Allan Massie, 5 September 1998
From the *Scotsman*
On Faulks's treatment of moral complexity

Yet, however powerful and engrossing, something is missing from the book. This is where the kind of 19th-century novel he has written fails Faulks. What one seeks for, and doesn't find, is a sense of moral complexity. Almost everybody in the novel is either good or bad: the choice between right and wrong is made very clear. But it wasn't like that in France then, and it shouldn't be like that in a novel. In short, this book is too simple-minded for the drama it seeks to portray, for the situation it sets out to examine.

Rosemary Goring, 23 August 1998
From *Scotland on Sunday*
On the theme of redemption

Though occasionally straining to add an explicit intellectual depth to his story, Faulks convincingly draws
together a complicated drama which puts historical
events and private histories alongside each other in
some sort of rationalising context. The importance of
integrity and self-knowledge is one of his themes,
underpinning tragedies and offering the hope of
redemption.

Faulks is good at redemption. His writing is rich
with compassion, and he offers it generously to all his
characters. By the end, there is no one, dead or alive,
left in the mire. This makes for satisfying storytelling,
but leaves an aftertaste of emotional manipulation, the
sense that ordinary, or extraordinary, lives have been
made to bear the weight of a philosophical exploration
rather than just unfold the way they normally do.

Alain de Botton, 22 August 1998
From the *Express*
On the character of Charlotte

Yet there is also a psychological richness here that most
thrillers lack. In only a few pages, Faulks manages to
convince the reader just why Charlotte would risk her
life for a pilot she has known for only a few days. And,
in Charlotte, Faulks has created a wonderfully capti-
vating heroine, with whom it is hard not to fall a little
in love (she seems to have a perfect blend of qualities:
beautiful but unselfconscious, inwardly passionate yet

outwardly reserved, romantic enough to write great love letters, but practical enough to parachute into France and deceive SS commanders). As readers of *Birdsong* will know, Faulks is also adept at writing some very superior sex scenes.

John Murray, 25 August 1998
From the *Independent on Sunday*
On Sebastian Faulks as a 'feminine' novelist

Faulks is a fine 'feminine' novelist in other respects. Like Mollie Keane, he is excellent at describing the interiors of both spacious mansions and untidy flats, and the minute details of women's clothes and make-up; he is also brilliant at evoking the guileless partying and light banter of young Londoners living in troubled times.

Barbara Trapido, 6 September 1998
From the *Observer*
On men and women, and Faulks's depiction of each

It is a pity for a book which evolves into a page-turner, and one peopled with some vivid minor characters, that *Charlotte Gray* begins so badly. Chapters one and four focus on Peter Gregory in flight and deal so relentlessly with Spitfires, Hurricanes, Lysanders and Typhoons that this reader longed for the livelier dialogue of Biggles. There is a lot of stuff about undercarriages, carburettors, altimeters and something called 'R/T'. Could there be a gender problem here, or is this a boring way to go on?

Now to the girl stuff. Chapters two and three belong

to Charlotte. We meet her at Waverley Station – just as in the *Lion d'Or* we so much more memorably meet Anne at the station in Janvilliers. Charlotte and Anne are in many ways comparable. Each is severed from a father ruined by active service, each works as a domestic servant in a crumbling French manor house inhabited by a sensitive, older Jewish man with a libertine, Parisian past, each sallies forth on a rickety bicycle, each has been formed by an experience of abandonment, though Charlotte's, disappointingly, is no more than an early example of the now fashionable False Memory Syndrome.

Robert Nye, 27 August 1998
From *The Times*
On men and women
Note: compare this extract with the previous one

Charlotte Gray begins with an excellently physical account of a solo bombing raid by a Hurricane over France at night, flown by a pilot called Peter Gregory. Then we are told of a young Scottish woman travelling south from Edinburgh by train, the eponymous heroine, and how she is casually recruited to work for a fictitious 'G Section' – a British organisation helping the Resistance. Charlotte meets and falls in love with Peter Gregory before undertaking her first mission. All this, it must be said, is very low-key.

David Robson, 30 August 1998
From the *Sunday Telegraph*
On genre categorisation

Charlotte, we discover, is not just a feisty young woman in love, but a daughter ensnared in a complex relationship with her father, an Edinburgh psychiatrist. The emotional damage suffered by her father in the First World War, and the knock-on effect on Charlotte, form a significant strand in the narrative, as well as providing the story with a moving denouement.

The Holocaust also casts a long shadow. In her effort to pass muster as a Frenchwoman, Charlotte enters the employment of a Jewish painter, who meets a predictably grisly fate. This strand of the narrative, too, is handled with skill and poignancy.

If the novel defies exact categorisation – is it a wartime romance, a thriller or a psychological mystery story? – that does not come across as a weakness. It merely testifies to the artistry of a novelist who is growing in authority with every book.

Hugo Barnacle, 23 July 1998
From the *Sunday Times*
On genre, style and the title of *Charlotte Gray*

There are two names on the cover and it is embarrassingly easy to imagine a lady novelist with a name like Charlotte Gray, writing a book with a title like Sebastian Faulks – he would be a faded rugger-playing socialite, probably in whom some lowly but startlingly attractive girl gradually discovers hidden depths – but, of course, there is no real scope for confusion because

Faulks is so well known as the author of *The Girl at the Lion d'Or* and *Birdsong. Charlotte Gray* follows these to complete a loose trilogy on French themes. This time the setting is the Second World War.

Anon, September 1998
From *Cosmopolitan*
On genre, style and audience
How far does this report represent the novel you have read?

BESTSELLER RATING: Very high. Faulks's last novel, *Birdsong*, sold 500,000 copies in the UK alone. This one could do even better.

WHAT'S IT ABOUT? A passionate love affair between two people torn apart by war.

UNPUTDOWNABLE? Definitely. This book has everything – a romantic backdrop, a cool glamorous heroine, a sexy, smouldering hero and an exciting plot involving wartime espionage. It just screams to be made into a film. All this, plus some of Faulks's most heartfelt, harrowing writing to date.

FAULKS TELLS *COSMO*:

'The book is the story of a young woman who copes with the legacy of sadness she's inherited by taking charge of her life. Even though she's beset by all kinds of danger, her progress is a triumphant one. It isn't really a war book in the same way *Birdsong* was; there's no actual fighting, although war is a background. I wanted to look at the insidious way that war affects individual lives.'

Glossary of literary terms

Alternating narratives When the narrative voice alternates between characters.

Bathetic Bathos is when an author employs trite sentimentality to manipulate reader's sympathies. The combining of formal literary styles with everyday subjects also creates bathos, or an anti-climax, e.g. 'Ne'er before had he seen/Such a lovely sweet wrapper/Of bright emerald green'.

Characterisation The way in which an author creates and then 'fleshes out' a character. Skilled fiction writers can create utterly believable characters through their choices of the characters' dress, speech and actions.

Climactic/Climax The climax of a novel is the moment of the highest drama and intensity. This moment involves the protagonist and usually heralds a turning point for the characters and/or plot.

Connotations The words or qualities which one word implies, e.g. Friday merely describes a day of the week, but the connotations of Friday could be party, weekend, relax, etc.

'Dead metaphor' When a metaphor has been so overused the phrase ceases to be figurative and takes on a literal meaning instead, e.g. the *eye* of a needle.

Denouement A French word meaning 'unknotting'. This refers to the unravelling of the plot – the solution to the mystery or the final explanation that is revealed.

Dramatic conflict When a conflict is set up within the narrative and must then be played out.

Eponymous heroine When a heroine has the same name as the novel's title, e.g. Jane Austen's *Emma*.

Euphemism When one term is substituted as a polite description for a cruder act, e.g. passing away instead of dying.

Fictional portrayal A description of make-believe events.

Fictive account An imaginary retelling of events.

Fictive narrative An imaginary story.

Fictive presentation An imaginary presentation of events.

Genre A category or type of literary work, e.g. novel, short story, poem etc. Genres can also be more specific – comedy, mystery, love story, etc.

Imagery The use of words to create pictorial images. Imagery often appeals to all the senses of taste, sight, touch and sound, and works on both literal and figurative levels.

Imaginative reality When reading a novel the reader enters into the 'imaginative reality' of the narrative. This is similar to the 'suspension of disbelief' theatre-goers engage in when seeing a play.

Innuendo When something is insinuated or implied.

Irony The discrepancy between the appearance of a situation and its reality. Irony can be verbal – e.g. when someone says, 'I'm *fine*' but means 'I'm angry' – or situational – e.g. a blind man who sells glasses. Dramatic irony is when the audience knows more than the characters.

Juxtapose When one event is positioned alongside another, usually with the intention of creating a literary link between the two, e.g. the birth of a baby and the simultaneous breaking of a vase.

Knowing narrative When the narrator and reader know more than the characters.

Linguistically Relating to language.

Metaphorical/Metaphor A figure of speech that ascribes the qualities (literally or imaginatively) of one thing to another, e.g. 'morning is a new sheet of paper for you to write on' – Eve Meriam

Narrating voice The voice of the narrator. This may be the voice of the main character or it may be the author's voice commenting upon the actions of the characters.

Narrative account A description given by the narrator.

Narrative ends The final destination towards which the narrative progresses.

Narrative method The method in which the author chooses to tell the story.

Narrative patterns The literary methods used that contribute towards the overall shape of the narrative, e.g. repetition can be used which can create a 'narrative pattern'.

Narrative shape The shape in which the narrative is constructed.

Narrative strategy The writing strategy or 'game plan' employed by an author. This determines when and how much information is given to the reader about both the characters and the plot.

Narrative structure The way in which the narrative is structured. A story can be told chronologically, using flashbacks, beginning at the end, etc.

Narrative styles The different narrative styles an author can use in order to manipulate the reader.

Narrative technique The different methods employed by an author in order to achieve his/her desired effect of the narrative upon the reader.

Omniscient narrator When the narrator has a godlike power of knowing and seeing all action, events and the characters' thoughts.

Overlapping narrative structure When the narrative is constructed so that certain events and/or characters' thoughts interweave and overlap throughout the narrative.

Paradoxically A paradox is a statement that is contradictory but ultimately true, e.g 'I never found a companion that was so companionable as solitude' – Henry David Thoreau

Pathetic Pathos is created when an audience feels genuine pity or sorrow for a sympathetic character.

Proleptic significance An event that will have great significance in the future, e.g. witnessing a crime at a young age could be proleptically significant to a character if they grew up to be either a criminal or a policeman.

Sonnet form A fourteen-line poem written using iambic pentameter.

Symbolise Symbolism is the use of words, characters, actions and objects that are to be understood literally but also represent higher, more abstract concepts, e.g. a caged bird can signify the literal fact of a bird in a cage as well as the symbolic values of lost freedom, feeling trapped, etc.

Tetralogy A collection of four dramatic works that are thematically linked.

Theme The central or overriding idea behind the story. The theme of a novel is often thought to contain the 'message' behind the work.

Third Person When a narrator tells the story from outside the narrative, yet also from a characters' perspective, e.g. Millie sat down weakly and thought, 'Well that's it then'.

Tone The attitude of the writing – be it carefree, formal, full of suspense, etc.

Tragedy A term applied to works in which events move to a fatal or disastrous conclusion.

Trilogy Any three literary or musical works that are thematically linked, e.g. the Greek tragedies *Oedipus Rex*, *Oedipus at Colonus* and *Antigone*.

Biographical outline

1953 20 April: Sebastian Charles Faulks born in Berkshire.

1966–71 Educated at Wellington College.

1974 Graduated from Emmanuel College, Cambridge.

1974–8 Became a teacher in London and wrote freelance articles for newspapers.

1978–81 Editor, New Fiction Society.

1978–82 Worked for *Daily Telegraph*.

1983–6 Feature editor, *Sunday Telegraph*

1984 *A Trick of the Light* published.

1986–9 Literary editor, *Sunday Telegraph*

1989 *The Girl at Lion D'Or* published.

1989–90 Deputy editor, *Independent on Sunday*.

1990–1 Associate editor, *Independent on Sunday*.

1992 *A Fool's Alphabet* published.

1992– Columnist, *Guardian*.

1993 *Birdsong* published.

1995 Made Fellow of the Royal Society of Literature. Named Author of the Year at the British Book Awards.

1996 *The Fatal Englishman*, triple biography of Christopher Wood, Richard Hillary and Jeremy Wolfenden, published.

1998 *Charlotte Gray* published.

2001 *On Green Dolphin Street* published.
2002 Film of *Charlotte Gray* released.
2002 Created CBE.

Select Bibliography

WORKS BY SEBASTIAN FAULKS

A Trick of the Light (Bodley Head, London, 1984)

The Girl at the Lion D'Or (Hutchinson, 1989); (Vintage, 1990)

A Fool's Alphabet (Hutchinson, 1992); (Vintage, 1993)

Birdsong (Hutchinson, 1993); (Vintage, 1994)

The Fatal Englishman (Hutchinson, 1996); (Vintage, 1997)

Charlotte Gray (Hutchinson, 1998); (Vintage, 1999)

With Jörg Hensgen *The Vintage Book of War Stories* (Vintage, 1999)

On Green Dolphin Street (Hutchinson, 2001); (Vintage 2002)

Also available in Vintage

Sebastian Faulks

A FOOL'S ALPHABET

'He is the best novelist of his generation' Allan
Massie, *Scotsman*

The events of Pietro Russell's life are told in 26 chapters. From A-Z each chapter is set in a different place and reveals a fragment of his story. As his memories flicker back and forth through time in his search for a resolution to the conflicts of his life, his story gradually unfolds.

'The uniqueness of his lovely, heartwarming novel is the way it plays with the arbitrariness of significance whilst telling the story of an uprooted life lived as a journey towards love and belonging'
Observer

'Sebastian Faulks's third and most magnificent novel is a "feel-good" experience from cover to cover'
Daily Mail

VINTAGE

Also available in Vintage

Sebastian Faulks

THE FATAL ENGLISHMAN
Three Short Lives

'Wildly exciting . . . it's a classic'
David Hard, *Spectator*

'Faulks's triple biography of three English prodigies who died young diligently sets each tragedy in its historical place and time to show how the feelings of a generation came to be projected upon their tragedy . . . Unusual, fascinating and interlocking in the oddest ways'
Brian Case, *Time Out*

'Superb . . . Faulks brings to these portraits the exquisite detail which made *Birdsong* so evocative. This is biography written with that revealing sense of the moment which marks good fiction . . . *The Fatal Englishman* is a mystery story of rare narrative power'
Jackie Wullschlager, *Financial Times*

VINTAGE

Also available in Vintage

Sebastian Faulks

ON GREEN DOLPHIN STREET

'Superbly done . . . another winner'
Sunday Telegraph

'A beautiful and moving love story'
Mail on Sunday

America, 1959, with two young children she adores and an
admired husband, Charlie, working at the British Embassy in
Washington, the world seems an effervescent place of parties,
jazz and family happiness to Mary van der Linden. But when
Frank, an American newspaper reporter, enters their lives they
are forced to confront the terror of the Cold War that is the
dark background of their carefree existence.

'A novel about adultery, jazz and alcohol . . . full of good
things, of the intensity of initially thwarted desire, of the
atmosphere of a new era coming alive, of the poignancy of
things past . . . Rings precisely true . . . Suave and fluent'
Sunday Times

'Both tense and affecting . . . At the end one releases the breath
one has unconsciously been holding, tribute to a writer of
considerable skill and ambition. A modern epic.'
Spectator

'Compelling . . . Faulks has become an international sensation'
Guardian

'An unparalleled, historical storyteller . . . An addictive romance
. . . beautifully evoked'
Daily Express

'He is the best novelist of his generation'
Allan Massie, *Scotsman*

BY SEBASTIAN FAULKS
ALSO AVAILABLE IN VINTAGE

❑	*The Girl at the Lion D'Or*	Sebastian Faulks	£6.99
❑	*A Fool's Alphabet*	Sebastian Faulks	£6.99
❑	*Birdsong*	Sebastian Faulks	£6.99
❑	*Tha Fatal Englishman*	Sebastian Faulks	£7.99
❑	*Charlotte Gray*	Sebastian Faulks	£6.99
❑	*The Vintage Book of War Stories*	Sebastian Faulks & Jörg Hensgen (eds)	£7.99
❑	*On Green Dolphin Street*	Sebastian Faulks	£6.99

- All Vintage books are available through mail order or from your local bookshop.
- Payment may be made using Access, Visa, Mastercard, Diners Club, Switch and Amex, or cheque, eurocheque and postal order (sterling only).

❑❑❑❑❑❑❑❑❑❑❑❑❑❑❑❑

Expiry Date:＿＿＿＿＿＿ Signature:＿＿＿＿＿＿＿＿＿＿＿＿＿

Please allow £2.50 for post and packing for the first book and £1.00 per book thereafter.

ALL ORDERS TO:
Vintage Books, Books by Post, TBS Limited, The Book Service,
Colchester Road, Frating Green, Colchester, Essex, CO7 7DW, UK.
Telephone:　(01206) 256 000
Fax:　　　　(01206) 255 914

NAME: ＿＿＿＿＿＿＿＿＿＿＿＿＿＿＿＿＿＿＿＿＿＿＿＿＿＿＿＿＿

ADDRESS: ＿＿＿＿＿＿＿＿＿＿＿＿＿＿＿＿＿＿＿＿＿＿＿＿＿＿

＿＿＿＿＿＿＿＿＿＿＿＿＿＿＿＿＿＿＿＿＿＿＿＿＿＿＿＿＿＿＿

＿＿＿＿＿＿＿＿＿＿＿＿＿＿＿＿＿＿＿＿＿＿＿＿＿＿＿＿＿＿＿

Please allow 28 days for delivery. Please tick box if you do not wish to receive any additional information.
Prices and availability subject to change without notice.　❑